1953–2003

GOLDEN YEARS

Calvin's First Half-Century
in the MIAA

David B. Tuuk

with Wallace Bratt

*To my old Pal
Tuuker
2005*

© 2005 Calvin Alumni Association
Calvin College, 3201 Burton St, Grand Rapids, Michigan, 49546-4388
All rights reserved.

Library of Congress Cataloging-in-Publication Data
ISBN 0-9703693-8-7
LCCN 2005921192

Cover design: Chris Stoffel Overvoorde

Contributing photographers: John Corriveau, Nathan Lujan, Dan Vos, Heritage Hall Archives

CONTENTS

DEDICATION

This book is dedicated to the following people and groups:

- All the athletes who participated on Calvin teams during the first 50 years of MIAA competition
- The coaches who gave many, many extra hours to fulfill their responsibility to the student athletes in their care
- Team managers, facilities custodians, grounds people, sports information directors, *Chimes* reporters, and everyone else who served in support functions
- The members of the various Calvin College administrations who budgeted the necessary funds for facilities, equipment, program maintenance, and travel
- Loyal alumni, donors, and fans who have consistently supported Calvin athletics

ACKNOWLEDGMENTS

This volume is a product of the collective efforts of many contributors. Special thanks is due the Calvin Alumni Association Board, which has generously agreed to sponsor its publication, and to Susan Buist and Mike Van Denend of the Alumni Office and my friend and colleague Wally Bratt, who have been enormously helpful in seeing this project to its completion.

The author also thanks Calvin presidents emeriti William Spoelhof and Anthony Diekema and current president Gaylen Byker for their contributions, as well as the MIAA officials, athletic directors, and coaches who sent their greetings and reflections. Among the colleagues, present and former Calvin coaches, and friends providing valuable information, pictures, and copy were the following: Dick Harms and the helpful staff of Calvin's Heritage Hall, MIAA publicist Tom Renner of Hope College, Gordon DeBlaey, Ed Douma, Dan Gelderloos, Ralph Honderd, Barb Keefer, Beverly Klooster, Nancy Meyer, Winnie Byker, Jeff Pettinga, Mary Schutten, Barney Steen, Jim Timmer, Sr., Kevin Vande Streek, Don Vroon, Dick Wilkins, Cindy Wolffis, Karla Wolters, Doris Zuidema, and Marv Zuidema. Jodie Bird and Natalie Hubers of the Physical Education Department willingly provided considerable secretarial assistance.

Deserving special thanks are Kim Gall, who graciously went many an extra mile in researching the history of various teams, and Jeff Febus, Calvin's sports information director, who provided much of the information found in Part Two of this volume. Bob Alderink of Calvin's Publishing Services patiently helped with innumerable details and did his usual excellent job with layout. Conrad Bult read through the entire manuscript and made helpful suggestions. Chris Stoffel Overvoorde designed the cover, and Susan Buist and Wally Bratt prepared the manuscript for publication.

The author warmly and sincerely thanks each of those noted above, as well as any other contributors whose names may have been inadvertently omitted from these lists.

David B. Tuuk

DAVID TUUK:
COACH, PROFESSOR, HISTORIAN, CALVIN FAN

Upon his retirement from teaching at Calvin in 1988, the tribute penned in his honor began as follows: "David Bruce Tuuk and Calvin College athletics: If you say one you think of the other."

It is impossible to improve on that introduction. For virtually his entire life, from sneaking into the Franklin campus gym as a youngster to combing the college archives for athletic history photographs in his retirement, Coach Tuuk has been engaged in the story of the Calvin Knights. (It is important to note he's been about much more than sports, as a faithful volunteer for numerous Kingdom ministries as well as one of the stalwarts of the Christian Reformed Recreation Center. How he found time to do all of this and be a great husband, father, and friend is a time management book waiting to be written.)

Officially, he served Calvin as a professor of physical education and coach for 36 years, from 1952 to 1988, but his legend as administrator, athletic director, NCAA tournament host, and Godfather of the Knights transcends his faculty tenure.

Thus it should come as no surprise that Coach Tuuk has now authored not one but two volumes on the history of Calvin athletics.

It is common to hear someone describe a Calvin Knights fan as "bleeding maroon and gold," but I believe Coach Tuuk is the only documented case. What makes the man even more remarkable is that this intense loyalty to alma mater never affected his strong sense of fair play and sportsmanship.

"He was a great coach, a real winner, but never lost sight of perspective or the true mission of Calvin," said "Ike" Isaac, an Albion College coach, on the occasion of Coach Tuuk's retirement. "Dave was tough, he continually sought after the truth, and life's real lessons were ever more a part of his philosophy and objectives."

In the research and writing of this book on Calvin's MIAA exploits, Coach Tuuk exhibited the foundational traits mentioned by Coach Isaac. He was unwavering in his quest to be fair and even-handed, spreading credit and kudos around—even as the ups-and-downs of Calvin sports history were documented with accuracy.

It is Coach Tuuk's fervent hope that this volume communicates an athletics program not only committed to excellence, but more importantly directed to building character and praising a faithful God. As in most of his efforts, I think he succeeded.

Thousands of Calvin athletes, the medal winners and the bench warmers alike, are grateful to Coach Tuuk for his development, care, and keeping of Calvin's great sports legacy. Coach, we salute you and thank you for being our Knight in Shining Armor.

Mike Van Denend

PURPOSE

For some 50 years, Calvin has been a member of the MIAA (Michigan Intercollegiate Athletic Association), the oldest collegiate athletic conference in the United States. As a result, thousands of students at Calvin have had the experience of being members of teams that competed against the other MIAA institutions, as well as a variety of other NCAA (National Collegiate Athletic Association) Division III schools throughout the country.

The purpose of this book is to recount in a general way the athletic activities that took place during this 50-year period. If unrecorded, this history obviously stands in danger of being permanently lost.

The first beneficiaries of this project will be former students who participated in the various sports, for whom memories of their involvement are supremely important. But others, too, will be interested in recounting and reviewing this history, among them the parents of athletes, alumni who have followed various teams, and a host of fans from Calvin's constituency. The college itself will also benefit from this narrative, since this brief history will of necessity acknowledge the vital role its administration has played in providing athletic facilities and coaches and meeting all the other needs of this large and complex program.

It is with a deep sense of loyalty that a group of emeriti have given themselves to the task of chronicling what went on during these 50 years.

CALVIN'S ENTRY INTO THE MIAA

In 1937 Calvin made its first overture to become a member of the MIAA (Michigan Intercollegiate Athletic Association). The league rejected that initial request, however, primarily because football wasn't included in Calvin's athletic program. That same year Calvin joined the MOCC (Michigan Ontario Collegiate Conference), a loosely organized league then made up of Lawrence Tech (Detroit), Adrian College, St. Mary's College (north of Detroit), Battle Creek College, Assumption College (Ontario), and Ferris Institute (Big Rapids). However, the MOCC disbanded after only five years. From 1942 until 1952 Calvin played as an independent institution, although some MIAA schools were regularly included on its schedules.

In 1952, during William Spoelhof's presidency, Calvin officials made another formal request for admittance to the MIAA. Professor Bud Hinga of Hope College served as Calvin's sponsor. After extended communication between President Spoelhof and the MIAA Board of Governors, Professor John DeVries, chair of the Athletics Committee, and Professor John Tuls were invited to meet with the MIAA board at its spring session at Albion College.

The minutes of the relevant portion of that meeting are in the right-hand column.

As the minutes imply, one school had voted against Calvin's entry. That dissenting voice joined the proponents of Calvin's entry in the subsequent voice vote, however, making the decision unanimous. Calvin was required to field teams in six of the seven sports on league schedules in the fall of 1953, necessitating the inauguration of cross country as a new Calvin sport.

That's how it all began.

Second Session, Thursday Evening
May 20, 1953

In addition to the directors listed for the afternoon meeting, Mr. John Fields, Alma College, and Professor Allen B. Stowe, Kalamazoo College, were also present. Mr. Fields assumed the chair.

As guests at the dinner and representing Calvin College at this meeting were Professors John DeVries and John Tuls.

The only topic of the evening meeting was discussion relative to the admittance of Calvin College as an eighth member of the Association. A period of time was allowed for an exchange of questions between the men representing Calvin College and those making up the Board of Directors. Following this initial discussion period Professors DeVries and Tuls retired from the room while the Board of Directors discussed the question at length among themselves and for a time with the Athletic Directors of the several colleges in attendance. After full discussion it was moved "that Calvin College be admitted to the Michigan Intercollegiate Athletic Association, the first year to be a probationary period." When put to vote by secret ballot a greater than 2/3rds majority was obtained in favor of admitting Calvin College to the Association, following which a unanimous decision was called for and obtained by voice vote. Calvin's representatives were then invited back to the meeting, informed of the action taken, and welcomed to participation in the Association.

The meeting was then adjourned until 10:00 a.m. Friday morning.

A GRATEFUL COLLEAGUE'S TRIBUTE TO BARNEY STEEN

It was my privilege to be appointed to the Physical Education Department at Calvin College in 1952. For a full year I "held the fort" in anticipation of the arrival of Barney Steen in 1953. I had first observed him many years before, since my family lived near the Franklin campus, where I had often seen him play basketball and baseball for the Knights.

Barney was a good fit at Calvin right from the start, and I gladly accepted my role as an assistant in the physical education and intercollegiate athletic programs. He was an easy person to get to know and understand.

Barney wanted to get started at once toward achieving the goals he had set for the department. He paid immediate attention to the minor program in physical education but soon realized that the general physical education program, which affected all students, also needed an overhaul. As a result of his efforts, "P.E." was made a requirement for everyone and was assigned academic credit. Intercollegiate athletics constituted another vast area that needed the immediate attention he gave it, especially with regard to the establishment of a perspective appropriate for Calvin's total educational mission.

Barney was fun to work with. He made decisions, was clear in his intentions, and got his point across with a kind spirit.

Years went by as we worked together and made progress in our relationships with the Calvin faculty and with MIAA personalities from other league institutions. We continued to look for better ways to serve the student body, and together we sought out better athletic facilities, which at that time were still rented. When Calvin bought the Knollcrest Farm, we started mulling over the facilities we would need, even dreaming at one point of moving the old Union Depot from its downtown location to Knollcrest for use as a fieldhouse! Ours was a close relationship, as we worked during those years to develop our department and its staff.

Barney Steen was also an astute, successful basketball coach who knew both how to plan and also how to implement that plan. He shared John Wooden's theory that "they will play only as well as they practiced." Barney, the consummate gentleman, was never known to "play the refs," as is common among some of today's coaches.

Designing the new Physical Education Building involved careful thought about educational philosophy and the role of physical education and intercollegiate sports at Calvin. Working long hours with architects from Perkins and Will, Barney guided the planning of a new structure that could accommodate a physical education program involving all students, but that also could serve as a facility for intramurals, athletic contests, and special events.

In sum, Dr. Barney Steen was the right man for the job and a "class act," when it came to developing a well thought out system in both physical education and athletics. He played a key role in the progress Calvin has made in both of these areas and became a valued, respected voice in the faculty. His thoughtful, considered approach was invaluable as we planned for the future.

I have utmost respect and admiration for my colleague, Dr. Barney Steen. It was an honor and a pleasure to serve with him at Calvin College.

David B. Tuuk

A TRIBUTE TO
DORIS ZUIDEMA

One year after her graduation from Calvin in 1962, Doris Zuidema was appointed to the Physical Education Department. During her undergraduate years she had been an active athlete, playing basketball for four years with the "Knighties," as the women's teams were then known, as well as participating in team archery and tennis. It was clear from this background that she was interested in sports and had athletic talent.

Ms. Zuidema joined the Calvin staff at a key moment in its history. Her coming coincided with the building of the new Physical Education Building, and the women's program was on the threshold of growth and development. Not only was she thrilled at the opportunity given her, but she also proved to have the gifts to capitalize on it, and all women's teams since that day have benefited richly from her contributions.

As the years passed, Zuidema became a master teacher both in the classroom and in developing athletic skills in Calvin women. For 13 years she guided the women's basketball program, but she was also called on at various times to coach archery, tennis, field hockey, and golf. In each of those sports she was a successful coach.

During the 1960s and 1970s Doris served as athletic director for the women's program. In addition, she became a prime mover in the AIAW (Association of Intercollegiate Athletics for Women), demonstrating superior leadership ability at the state level of the organization and thereby helping to open new opportunities for women in sports.

Anyone observing Coach Zuidema throughout the years soon came to see that student athletes had great respect for her, both as a coach and as an administrator. During her long tenure at Calvin she, for her part, enjoyed the satisfaction of seeing the quality of women's athletics improve dramatically.

When in 1978 the women's program was merged with that of the men in a new, unified MIAA, Doris was once again called on to fulfill leadership roles. As time passed, she successfully led Calvin in the introduction of several new women's sports, among them cross country, swimming, track and field, golf, and soccer. Her counterparts at other MIAA institutions were among the first to appreciate the sterling quality of her contributions.

The caliber of women's athletic programs at Calvin today is directly attributable to her leadership, devotion, imagination, and hard work. Ms. Zuidema had an excellent relationship for over three decades not only with hundreds of student-athletes but also with her grateful colleagues. It is with pride that we as staff salute her as coach, professor, administrator, and friend.

David B. Tuuk

THREE CALVIN COLLEGE PRESIDENTS REFLECT ON CALVIN AND THE MIAA

Dr. William Spoelhof
President of Calvin (1951-1976)

One of the missions of my administration was to broaden Calvin's base. The college had been very exclusive of the outside and inclusive of the inside. I believed it was important to change that emphasis so that Calvin would become better known beyond the Christian Reformed Church and its constituents.

My administration's attempts in that direction were helped in those early years by joining the Michigan Colleges Foundation, for example. This organization was composed of a group of Protestant-based colleges in Michigan. In partnership with businessmen, it helped raise money for the various Michigan colleges.

This same desire to make Calvin better known was one reason for joining the MIAA as well. But my administration had yet another reason. The intense rivalry between Hope and Calvin had existed for many years. Rightly or wrongly, we judged that joining a league would help soften it somewhat.

Calvin's winning of the MIAA men's basketball championship already in 1953-54, the first year of its membership in the conference, meant that our team was to participate in a playoff game with Lawrence Tech for the state championship of the NAIA, of which we were a member at the time. If Calvin won this game, the team would go on to Kansas City and be obliged to play on Sunday. This was the one time I prayed for our team to lose a ball game. They did.

Dr. Anthony J. Diekema
President of Calvin (1976-1995)

The fact that, as a student, I played basketball both before and after Calvin became a member of the MIAA gave me a firsthand perspective on participating both outside and within a league context. I found Calvin's joining the MIAA to be a positive step for student-athletes primarily because it gave competition a more meaningful context. Before league membership we measured each game independently, and results had only

Diekema drives to the basket.

limited significance for the future. Nor did those games give a clear indication as to where we stood in relation to peers and peer colleges. That all changed soon after we entered the league—and won our first championship. Playing within the context of the MIAA also had a positive effect on student morale and communal esprit de corps.

My appreciation of the MIAA continued after I became Calvin's president. For the most part, I thoroughly enjoyed my associations with the MIAA and my presidential colleagues. Much of that was because we all embraced a similar philosophy of the place of athletics within a liberal arts educational environment. All of us viewed student-athletes as students first and athletes second.

Calvin often played a leadership role in keeping this philosophy at the forefront. The fact that the MIAA cherishes true amateurism in athletics has set the league and its institutions apart from many others over time. The pervasive philosophy that underscored the integral and positive relationship between athletics and education made dealing with the "nuts and bolts" of the league and setting priorities much easier. Working as president within the context of the MIAA was a pleasant experience for me.

Dr. Gaylen Byker
President of Calvin
(1995-present)

Calvin College has benefited greatly from its half-century of membership in the MIAA. However, we like to think the MIAA has benefited from Calvin's membership, too. I find the conference and the college to be good fits for one another.

The league's mission statement shows this symmetry clearly, for it resonates well with Calvin's philosophy of intercollegiate athletics. We affirm two basic principles, as that statement enunciates them. First, we agree that primary considerations in all conference decisions are the welfare of every participating student-athlete, the academic missions of member colleges, and fair play at all conference events. Second, we affirm the policy by which the governance of intercollegiate athletics at member colleges ultimately rests with the college presidents.

Byker prepares for a match.

It has been a wonderful experience to be in a conference that recognizes that college athletics are part of the broader picture of liberal arts education. What a pleasure it is to be part of a league that can use the term *student-athlete* and have it mean something! With membership in the MIAA, Calvin College participates in a conference that takes athletics seriously (after all, we keep score) but puts them in context. We are proud to be members of a league that annually sees its student-athletes graduate on time and go on to great careers and graduate schools. We are privileged to be joined with a conference in which All-Americans and Academic All-Americans are named with equal frequency.

Benediction

Numbers 6:24-26 NIV

"The LORD bless you

and keep you:

the LORD make his face

shine upon you

and be gracious to you;

the LORD turn his face

toward you and give

you peace."

PART ONE

**50 YEARS OF
INTERCOLLEGIATE SPORTS
AT CALVIN**

1953-2003

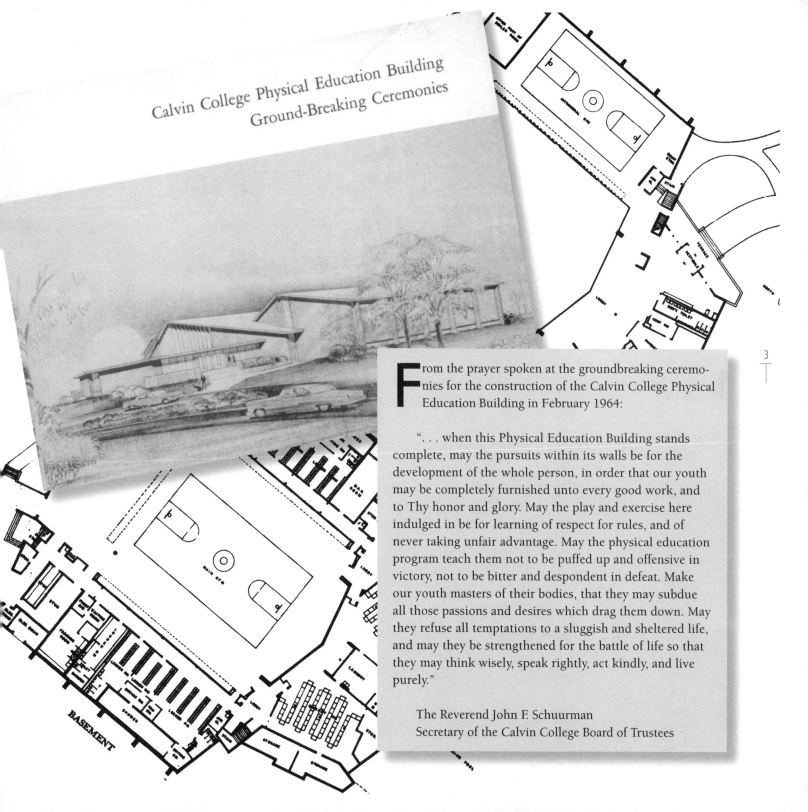

Calvin College Physical Education Building
Ground-Breaking Ceremonies

From the prayer spoken at the groundbreaking ceremonies for the construction of the Calvin College Physical Education Building in February 1964:

". . . when this Physical Education Building stands complete, may the pursuits within its walls be for the development of the whole person, in order that our youth may be completely furnished unto every good work, and to Thy honor and glory. May the play and exercise here indulged in be for learning of respect for rules, and of never taking unfair advantage. May the physical education program teach them not to be puffed up and offensive in victory, not to be bitter and despondent in defeat. Make our youth masters of their bodies, that they may subdue all those passions and desires which drag them down. May they refuse all temptations to a sluggish and sheltered life, and may they be strengthened for the battle of life so that they may think wisely, speak rightly, act kindly, and live purely."

The Reverend John F. Schuurman
Secretary of the Calvin College Board of Trustees

WOMEN'S ARCHERY

1953-1959 Increasingly on Target

Archery was never a high-profile sport at Calvin, but during the nearly three decades of its existence it provided a significant number of Calvin women with a challenging outlet and a variety of interesting experiences.

Since in the 1950s Calvin was still located on the crowded, overtaxed Franklin campus, the team had to look elsewhere for practice facilities. The only suitable area the squad was able to find was in the Franklin Park Lodge.

Despite such limitations, Calvin's women did experience at least one moment of remarkable success in those early years. In the spring of 1959 the team of Agnes Boogerd, Georgene Ludemann, and Bev Klooster shot three Columbia rounds from the designated 30-, 40-, and 50-yard distances, two on a Friday and the third the following Saturday. At that time, shooting was done with straight bows and without special guides or sighting devices.

To everyone's surprise, including their own, the Calvin women won the WMIAA runner-up trophy that year. Bev Klooster continues to attribute that fine achievement to Agnes Boogerd, insisting that the team won the trophy only "because Agnes was such a good shot. She carried the rest of us to the score we had."

This early progress proved to serve the Calvin team well in the next decade.

1960-1969 Aiming High

During the time archery was a WMIAA sport, the equipment that the archers used changed dramatically. In the 1950s they used primitive bows, the kind generally available to all physical education students. In order to hit the target, archers had to find an aim point high above the target, since the arrow dropped significantly during its flight. As the style of the bow changed, so did the way in which archers aimed. Coach Doris Zuidema introduced the use of map pins stuck on strips of tape applied to the inside of the bow, with one pin indicating 30 yards, another 40, and the third 50. Later, sighting devices were mounted on the inside of the bow, stabilizers were affixed to hold the bow steady, and a mechanism allowing for uniform string pressure was developed. All three of these improvements resulted in increased accuracy.

Especially in the second half of the new decade, Calvin experienced sterling success. Coach Zuidema's team won

Lois Hoving

its first WMIAA championship in 1966. Mary Wynbeek was the tournament's individual high scorer in both 1966 and 1967 and was the first Calvin archer to win the Jo Dunn Outstanding Archer Award for Sportsmanship and Marksmanship. Lois Hoving won the award in 1968 and led the team to its second championship in 1969.

1970-1982 Good Sportsmanship Despite a Lost Sport

Calvin continued to compete successfully in archery over the next 12 years. The squad won the tournament twice, in 1970 and again in 1976. Three Knight archers won the Jo Dunn Award during the 1970s: Sheryl Hondorp in 1972, Joan Kooi in 1973, and Cathy Youngsma in 1976.

Archery was discontinued at Calvin and other MIAA colleges in 1982. As time went on, the gap left by its demise was filled by the steady development of a number of new sports for women.

STRAY ARROWS

Since it was not common for students to come to Calvin with previous archery experience, Coach Doris Zuidema was forced to recruit her squad from her basketball team. Early spring practice, before the winter weather broke, was held in Room P300 in the Physical Education Building. Before beginning their actual shooting, the archers stacked the chairs in the back corners of the room, thus creating a free space 30 yards long.

Since many team members were "archers in the rough," arrows frequently went astray. Coach Jim Timmer tells of going to teach a class in Room 300 one day, only to find a variety of arrows protruding from the ceiling and walls at a number of interesting angles. It was Calvin's version of the "Old West," straight from the "Midwest."

6

MEN'S BASEBALL

1954-1959 *Batter Up!*

Barney Steen, who had played baseball during his student days in the late 1930s and early 1940s, coached the first Calvin team to compete within the framework of the MIAA. Between the end of World War II and Calvin's admission to the league in 1953, the Knights had played a number of MIAA schools, but the 1954 season constituted, in a sense, a new beginning.

Calvin's home field, such as it was, was a sandy diamond in Franklin Park, southwest of the campus. The field had no fences; if a ball was hit sharply between the outfielders, it kept rolling almost indefinitely through the sparse grass and rich crop of sand burrs, usually resulting in a home run. On occasion, home games were also played at Richmond Park or at Valley Field on Grand Rapids' west side. Sites for away games were often no better, of course. All in all, the baseball program was relatively spare back then. Calvin's teams of the early 1950s never would have dreamed of the luxury of a trip south; they contented themselves instead with spring practice in the basement gymnasium of the Franklin dorm, with baseballs flying in all directions.

Herm Kolk, Pete Van Vliet, and John DeMey constituted the Knights' pitching staff for that first league season. DeMey had played on the 1953 team and was a proverbial "fireballer," throwing a fastball that undoubtedly would have registered in the 90s, if today's measuring devices had been available back then. Gord DeKruyter was catcher, and Norm DeNooyer and Mike Vanden Bosch played the outfield and provided solid hitting power. Vanden Bosch was the first Calvin base stealer to use the head-first slide, while DeNooyer became the team's first All-MIAA player. The 1954 season saw the Knights attain a respectable 12-10 overall record, although they went only 3-6 in league play.

John DeMey

The 1955 squad fared less well, winning eight games while losing twelve, and having minimal success against MIAA teams. A split with Hope was one of the few consolations the season provided. The team was not without its hitters, however. Ohio native Stan Holthouse batted .368 and earned a place on the All-MIAA squad, while Chuck Witteveen hit .379 and Don Vroon batted .289. A major reason for the team's disappointing performance was the loss of pitcher John DeMey, who had left for two years in the army.

The following season saw more effective play by the Knights, as the team ended its MIAA schedule in third place. Two players stood out that year. The first was John Kloosterman, who batted an impressive .495; the second was Arnie Rottman, noted for both his fielding wizardry at first base and for his hitting skills, which were reflected in his .395 average.

The 1957 squad, helped significantly by the return from military service of John DeMey, enjoyed a winning 8-6 league season. In addition to DeMey, key players in the Knights' third-place finish were pitcher Karl DeJonge and veteran hitters Norm DeNooyer and Mike Vanden Bosch, along with newcomer Dick Katte. The '57 season was more enjoyable for the team partly because more home games were played at Valley Field, which had superior facilities.

The following season was average; one of its few high points was the selection of John DeMey to the all-league roster. Nor did the Knights fare better in 1959. They lost the first 10 games they played, managing to salvage the season only by taking two games from Albion and then defeating Grand Rapids Junior College and Aquinas in the final games on their schedule.

In sum, although Calvin baseball had its bright spots in the 1950s, it enjoyed, by and large, only modest success.

1960-1969 From Struggle to Strength

Not surprisingly, the 1960 season also proved to be lackluster, its only shining moment being pitcher Art Kraai's election to the all-league team. The season also was the last for

MOTHER'S "HARDT ATTACK"

After two years in the army, I returned to Calvin in the spring of 1956 and resumed pitching for the baseball team for both the '57 and '58 seasons.

On a beautiful afternoon at Franklin Park in the spring of 1958, my parents, who had never before witnessed a Calvin game, were in attendance, along with my wife, Marcia, and infant daughter, Julie.

One of my times at bat I made solid contact with a fastball and drove it deep, over the left fielder's head. Since Franklin Park had no outfield fence, I legged around the bases, while the fielder gave chase to the ball. The play at home plate was close, but head first, I slid safely home in a cloud of dust.

As I got up, breathlessly dusted myself off, and examined my scraped and bleeding elbows and chin, my 68-year-old mother, in her delightful Dutch brogue, exclaimed to my wife, "Och, I never again come to one of dees baseball games! For sure I taught bodt John und me vould haf un hardt attack."

John DeMey

Barney Steen, whose demanding duties as basketball coach and athletic director made it necessary that he give up his position in baseball. Don Vroon, who had played for Steen in the 1950s, was named Calvin's new coach.

Despite the enthusiasm he brought to the task and the development of a new home diamond, Vroon's first three years were difficult. His 1961 team, though playing many

CHAIN GANG

On occasion, Coach Steen had a fertile imagination when it came to devising schemes for getting his basketball players in condition in the fall.

Calvin's new baseball diamond had been roughed in during the summer of 1961, but it needed a lot of additional work. For one thing, the soil was infested with thousands of stones that had to be picked up before the field could be completed. Another challenge for Coach Steen.

The solution was simple. Steen had Coach Vroon mount a small garden tractor equipped with a trailer and slowly criss-cross the field, while the basketball team followed close, bending over to pick up the stones and then tossing them into the trailer. Whether the exercise had aerobic value remains dubious, but it got the job done.

close games, ended with a disastrous 1-21 record. Dan Bos batted .302 and Jim Timmer .250, but the team batting average was a woeful .184, and Walt Dahnke was the sole pitcher to win a game. Yet, despite all odds, Vroon somehow managed to hold things together.

The next season's team batting average moved up slightly, to .218, but there was no improvement at all in the squad's win-loss record, as it went 1-16 overall and failed to win a single league game. Slight progress marked the '63 effort, as Calvin won three games, lost 13, and tied one—a game with Hope. All three victories were against MIAA opponents.

The next three seasons were a happier story. The 1964 squad won twelve games while losing only seven, going 7-5 in the MIAA and finishing in third place. Standout pitcher

Ken Fletcher from Kalamazoo had a 3-1 league record and a fine 1.45 ERA. Phil Van Slooten played a capable second base and batted .387 to win a place on the all-league team, while John Rozeboom hit .351. The 1965 team saw similar success, winning as many games as it lost. Four pitchers won two games apiece, and Jon Mulder, a freshman, hit .480 overall and .425 in the MIAA, gaining a spot on the all-league team in the process.

In 1966, Vroon's last year as baseball coach, Calvin took second place in the league, its highest finish since entering the MIAA some 13 years before. Two pitchers stood out. Ken Brinks went 3-0 in the league and compiled an imposing 1.29 ERA; Click Groot also won three games, while losing only once. The Knights' offense was led by Jon Mulder, who hit .387, and Jim Goorman, whose batting average was .344 and who was named to the All-MIAA squad. Vroon's final year was a satisfying one.

Jim Czanko, a new member of the physical education staff, succeeded Vroon in 1967. His first team compiled an 8-11 record overall and won four league games while losing eight. Although the Knights dropped to sixth place in the league, their pitching gave reason for optimism. Click Groot and Bruce Bode were reliable starters, and freshmen Jerry Koster and Paul Milkamp showed promise for the future. Leading hitters were Bill Brashler, a talented catcher with a .322 average, Gerry Buurma, who batted .328, and Buzz Wynbeek, who also hit .328. Jim Goorman and Mickey Phelps anchored the infield.

A measure of the promise shown in 1967 was realized in 1968, as Czanko's team split in both its overall and MIAA record. Bruce Bode and Jerry Koster each won three games, while talented sophomore Paul Milkamp ended the season with a 4-2 record. Paul Veltman also provided pitching help. Mickey Phelps had a fine year as he batted .353, and Buzz Wynbeek was chosen for the All-MIAA team.

The team continued to mature in 1969, as Czanko guided the Knights to a second-place finish in the MIAA, immediately behind Albion. Ken Post did a superb job behind the plate, and Calvin's strong pitching staff, composed of

COACH WHO?

Don Vroon, a taskmaster with great plans for improving our win-loss record, was Calvin's baseball coach during the 1963 season. However, we weren't very good. Our chief strength, such as it was, had nothing to do with the game; rather, it lay in the unpredictable, irrepressible spirit of several team members.

One day, halfway through the tense first game of a double-header in Kalamazoo, the umpire ejected Coach Vroon for making an excessively vigorous protest. Since Vroon had no assistant, coaching duties theoretically fell to our team captain and center fielder.

Vroon, not readily discouraged, devised a way to continue to direct the team himself. He took his stand beyond the board fence in center field and issued directives through the fence to the team captain, who then relayed them to the bench.

However, he hadn't reckoned with his squad's free spirits, most notably Rich Rienstra, who decided to make his own decisions. One of them was to call a timeout, stride to the mound in classic Stengelese fashion, and insert "Posthole Pete," a freshman who wasn't even a pitcher, into the game as a reliever. As Vroon, his baseball cap frantically bobbing up and down just above the level of the fence, screamed, "What's he doing?" and both benches were convulsed with laughter, Rienstra stood knowingly alongside the mound and in mock seriousness instructed the novice Posthole Pete about wind-up and stretch procedures. Calvin quite predictably lost the game, 9-3, but it had been great fun for everyone—except Coach Vroon.

Jim Timmer, Sr.

Bruce Bode, Jerry Koster, Paul Milkamp, and Tom Steen, gave Czanko consistently reliable performances. Second baseman Jim Tuinstra and shortstop Mickey Phelps provided stability in the infield, while Wynbeek and Jim Kett played a steady game in the outfield.

Although Coach Czanko decided to leave Calvin and accept the position of athletic director at the new Kentwood High School at the end of the season, he had the satisfaction of seeing distinct improvement in the baseball program during his three-year tenure.

1970-1979 Solid Success, Occasional Slumps

A new decade brought with it a new coach, as Marvin Zuidema replaced Czanko. Zuidema's first season was, in some sense, a surprise. Given the solid squad of 1969 and the return of many veteran players, the team's winning 11-10 record might have been expected. However, the Knights surprised everyone by winning their first MIAA baseball championship as well, with seven wins and three losses. Paul Milkamp pitched very well, as did John Evenhouse, who turned in an exceptional 1.40 ERA in eight games. All-MIAA shortstop Phelps, who was also named league MVP, led a solid team effort and was joined by Buzz Wynbeek, Dick Hatfield, Bill Bulthuis, and Darl Pothoven, who consistently delivered key hits. This unanticipated championship provided Zuidema with an auspicious start as baseball coach.

The 1971 season was also very satisfying, as Calvin, with a 9-3 record, shared a co-championship with Albion. Evenhouse continued his stellar pitching and was backed up by Mark Joosse. Both Evenhouse and Dick Hatfield made the All-MIAA squad, the latter on the basis of his exceptional hitting.

Although the following year did not bring a third league championship, the Knights played well. They closed the 1972 season with an 8-12 record overall, but with a winning percentage in the MIAA, having defeated their opponents seven times, while losing five games. All but one of the non-conference losses were to larger schools such as Central Michigan

University, Eastern Michigan, and Ferris State. As expected, John Evenhouse led Knight pitchers with a 6-4 record, while left hander Wayne Schaap finished the year with a very credible four wins and four losses. Dick Hatfield, with his .345 batting average, once again provided considerable offensive power, while Darl Pothoven hit a respectable .250.

Though led by four seniors and four juniors, Calvin's 1973 team was a mild disappointment, as the team compiled a 5-13 record overall, winning only three conference games. The 1974 squad showed a bit more strength, winning five league games and losing seven. Tom Visser and Randy Wolthuis were Calvin's leading pitchers; Visser's ERA for the season was 3.69, just slightly better than Wolthuis' 3.87. The Knights' hitters were led by Jeff Sage, with a .385 average, and Jim Unrath, who batted .333. At the close of the season Sage and Gerry Sikkenga were named to the All-MIAA team.

1975 proved to be a banner year, as Calvin improved significantly, winning the MIAA championship with an 8-3 record. Its overall record of 13-6 also was better than that of the previous year. Strong pitching helped Calvin's cause immeasurably. Dave Neher was perfect in terms of wins and losses, going 4-0; Randy Wolthuis won four games while losing only once; Tom Visser compiled an incredible 0.67 ERA in 40 innings, an achievement that placed him second among all-time MIAA pitchers; and freshman Jack Tuuk went 3-1, striking out 33 batters in 21 innings of work. Rog King led the team with a .326 batting average, and Tom Ellens hit .306; Gerry Sikkenga and Jim Te Bos also were productive hitters. Randy Wolthuis and Jim DeGroot received all-league recognition at the season's close; Wolthuis also was named the MIAA's MVP.

Although the 1976 squad won more games than it lost overall, its final conference record stood at 6-6. Joining veteran pitchers Tuuk, Visser, and Neher was Brian Ellens. The following year, with virtually the same pitchers, the team again achieved a 6-6 league performance, but it managed only one victory against non-MIAA opponents. Jim Unrath, Brian Sikkenga, and Randy Baker were responsible for the bulk of the squad's offense.

1978 saw a coaching change, as Jeff Pettinga was named Zuidema's replacement. Pettinga was an enthusiastic leader and a knowledgeable strategist. His enthusiasm proved to be contagious; after the two years he devoted primarily to organizing the program, his team took the MIAA championship in 1980.

Because of the nature of the sport, the length of Pettinga's coaching career, and the space available, the only seasons to be reviewed in greater detail will be those in which Calvin won the league championship. This emphasis is not in any way meant to downgrade the efforts of the many additional players who trained hard, competed well, and made Calvin a force in the MIAA, though never enjoying participation on a championship squad. The Calvin community respects them all and hopes that they, too, continue to enjoy many positive memories of their years of playing, including their spring break trips to the South.

Only after he had led the program for 27 years, the longest tenure achieved by any Calvin baseball coach, did Pettinga retire. The stability of Calvin's program is an enduring tribute to him and to and his leadership, as are the outstanding facilities that have been developed at Calvin during his career, including, among other things, a carefully groomed playing field, a bullpen for pitcher warm-up, and a batting cage. Calvin's baseball facilities rank with the state's best among Division III schools.

The 1980 Co-Championship: Fastballs, Curves, Veterans, Newcomers

The 1980 season, Pettinga's third, brought Calvin's fourth league championship since its entrance into the MIAA, as it tied with Alma for the conference title. One factor in the team's success was its combination of experienced players and gifted, dedicated newcomers, with both groups contributing significantly the total effort.

Sophomore Jim Snoeyink, who had not tried out for baseball during his first year at Calvin, but who threw an excellent fastball and an outstanding curve, led the all-important pitching staff. Second to him and sharing pitching duties during double headers was Mark Van Meeteren, a transfer from Grand Rapids Community College. Van Meeteren, too, had a fine fastball; a second facet of his strength was his ability to spot his pitches with unusual accuracy.

The 1980 team also featured a solid defense led by catcher Bob Tuuk, shortstop Russ Rykse, third baseman Scott Hamstra, and second baseman Mark Zietse. Hamstra and Zietse became all-conference players, but the work of Tuuk and Rykse also was invaluable throughout the season.

Depth at the plate and in the outfield was provided by Mark Stob, Randy Stout, Mark Ekdom, and Curt Malling, with Stout and Stob becoming All-MIAA selections. Left-handed batter Randy Hazenberg was the squad's able designated hitter.

Bench strength provided by Keith Saagman, Jeff Schuiteman, Steve Kraai, and Brent Wassink was decisive in the team's championship run. Only by virtue of the cooperation of all these players did the 1980 championship become a reality.

One, Two, Three Strikes—and In: The 1984 Championship Team

The 1984 squad has the distinction of being the first Calvin baseball team to be selected to play in the NCAA tournament. The Knights were undisputed conference champions, and on the basis of their record and the strength of their schedule, they were invited by the regional committee to participate in the tournament.

Unusually good depth in pitching was the hallmark of the '84 Knights. John Collier, a transfer student from Grand Valley State University, was the team's number-one pitcher, was undefeated in the conference, and was selected the league's most valuable player. Ken Vermeulen was a solid second pitcher, with Jeff Mast, Tim Montsma, and Scott Koster giving additional depth. The team's relief specialist was Brad Sims.

Calvin's excellent infield included Tim Montsma, Kevin Van Duyn, Jim Schipper, and Tim Zietse, while Joe Rinckey was catcher. The tandem of Van Duyn and Schipper has a unique place in Calvin baseball history in that both of them started as freshmen and were an outstanding double-play combination for four consecutive years. A tribute to their skill was the fact that they were recognized as all-conference players from 1984 to 1986. Van Duyn won all-league honors the next year as well and was the first Calvin player to be named NCAA All-Region and All-American. Tim Montsma also was selected for the All-MIAA squad.

Doug Ybema, John Huizinga, and Greg "Moses" Malone played the outfield and made significant contributions with both their bats and throwing arms. For his achievements Huizinga received all-league recognition.

The trip to the NCAA playoffs began and ended at Ohio Northern University. The Knights lost their first two games but came away having learned valuable lessons in how to play championship baseball. The first loss was to Marietta College, which had an exceptionally strong Divison III program, while the second was at the hands of New York State College at Oswego.

Coach Pettinga remembers the 1984 team for its response to tough situations. Its remarkable achievements are reflected in the fact that eight of its players were named to either the first- or second-team all-conference squad.

Back on Top—16 Years Later

Since winning its second championship under Pettinga in 1984, the Knights played consistent baseball and frequently were the runner-up in the conference. Only in 2000, however, did they meet their goal of winning another league title.

Due to the new MIAA format introduced in 1984 that involved three-game weekend series against each conference school, the pitching staff needed to expand. Equal to the challenge was the starting rotation of Mike Ott, Aaron Wiers, and Ryan Wolthuis, with all three of them receiving All-MIAA recognition. Andy Miedema provided short relief, while Matt Schmitz was the team's long reliever.

When not pitching, Aaron Wiers played a fine first base; he also was an excellent hitter. His selection as MIAA MVP in both 2000 and 2001 makes him one of the very few athletes in the conference's history to be accorded that honor in baseball twice. Dirk Eppinga was the team's designated hitter and played first base when Wiers was pitching. Third baseman Justin Cole joined Eppinga as an all-conference selection.

Two outfielders, Ross Hunderman and Steve Ekkens, also achieved all-league status. Together with Jason TeBos and utility outfielder Andrew Drake, they provided much of the team's offensive power.

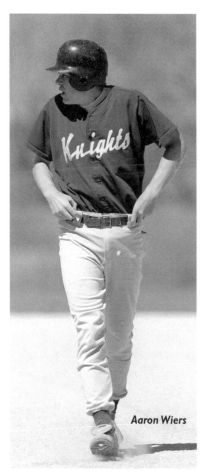

Aaron Wiers

By virtue of its first place finish in the MIAA, Calvin was once again selected for participation in the NCAA tournament to be played in Canton, Ohio. Losses to Ohio Wesleyan and the College of Mount St. Joseph did not lessen the satisfaction of an excellent season.

Stealing Home: The 2002 Championship Run

The 2002 season proved to be particularly exciting. Playing a 40-game schedule, Calvin won 28 times, setting a school record for single-season victories in the process. 2002 was the third consecutive year the Knights won more than 20 games.

Members of that team will not soon forget the way the

Jim Deters

season ended. Hope came into the decisive final regular season series with a 26-game winning streak and a perfect 15-0 record in the league. Calvin's MIAA record was 13-2. In order to win the conference championship, the Knights would have to sweep the series. And they did—in exhilarating fashion.

Mike Ott, Jim Deters, and Andy Miedema were the team's starting pitchers; Matt Schmitz also started on occasion, but he specialized in long and short relief. All three primary starters received either first- or second-team league honors. On the basis of his eight wins, a league record, as well as his 66 strikeouts, Deters was named the conference's MVP and was granted all-regional recognition.

The starting infield consisted of old, new, and transplanted players who changed positions. Senior captain Ben Dykhouse was catcher, and co-captain Mark Jansen was at second base. Among the transplants, Darrell Heuker made a successful switch from catching to first base, and Mike Noorman, a former shortstop, proved to be an effective third baseman. Freshman Josh Vriesman did an outstanding job playing shortstop. Dykhouse, Heuker, and Vriesman were named to the All-MIAA honor squad. Three outstanding sophomores—Terry O'Neal, Bryce Weston, and Aaron Griffith—did an excellent job in the outfield.

By virtue of their conference championship, the Knights were given an automatic berth in the NCAA playoffs at the University of Wisconsin–Oshkosh. Losing their first two games to Lakeland College and the University of Wisconsin–Stevens Point, they returned home once again winless, but with an eye to better things in the future.

WOMEN'S BASKETBALL

1953-1959 *Courting Excellence*

Basketball was not yet part of the WMIAA program when Calvin began league play in 1953. However, the "Knighties," as the women's basketball team was called back then, did play a regular schedule with distinction and deserve to be mentioned in this brief history.

Dave Tuuk coached the team for a second consecutive year during the 1953 season. The squad did very well, as it won the Grand Rapids City Recreation's "Pin-up League" championship. Its only outside competition was furnished by Hope College. The game with Hope was played in Holland, and Calvin's women won by a resounding 35-15 score.

The following year Nell Oosthoek, a member of the previous year's championship team and a graduate of the class of 1954, was appointed to head the women's program. Coach Oosthoek did an outstanding job, leading her teams to three straight championships in the city league. Among the notable aspects of her tenure was the 24-game winning streak her talented squads compiled. Back then, basketball was still played on a divided court, with three forwards on offense and three defensive players deployed across the center line.

Another high point of those years, in addition to the championships, was a trip the team took to East Lansing, where Calvin's women defeated both Michigan State University and Olivet College. On a less competitive note, the team also participated in a WMIAA play day in 1956. A play day was a low-key experience that was more recreational than competitive in character. At times teams from participating schools would even exchange some of their players, simply for fun and fellowship. The second team sport included in the play day program was volleyball, while table tennis and badminton were offered on an individual basis. At the close of the 1956-57 school year, Coach Oosthoek left her position for graduate study at the University of Michigan, having imprinted a mark of excellence on Calvin's program.

The following year Ellen Rottman assumed responsibility for the women's team. The Knighties continued their excellent play, going undefeated in the City League with a 9-0 record, following which they represented Grand Rapids in the state basketball tournament held in Flint. Coach Rottman's squad advanced as far as semi-final play, when they were defeated, 32-25, by Kalamazoo.

A succcessful innovation instituted by Rottman was the

DANIELLE AND GOLIATH

In the 1960s and early 1970s, the Calvin women's basketball squad was not easily intimidated, readily taking on teams from major universities—and with remarkable success. Between 1965 and 1971 the Lady Knights defeated Western Michigan University in five of six games played, once by a score of 61-16! Central Michigan they bested in four of seven contests. The Lady Knights won all four games with Eastern Michigan and defeated Michigan State University four times in six attempts.

With the passage of Title IX in 1974, the larger schools began to invest more money into their women's programs. Calvin put these universities on its schedule through 1979, but then stopped doing so, since the Lady Knights could no longer compete with them. Athletic scholarships made the difference.

development of a two-team system, the "Knighties" and the "Dayzies," both of which played in the City League. An obvious advantage of the set-up was that it eliminated the tough job of cutting players from the team. The second squad, the "Dayzies," proved its mettle by winning the league "B" championship, thus giving Coach Rottman a sweep in city competition. Calvin clearly had become one of the top teams in the Grand Rapids area.

1960-1969 No Let-Up

For roughly the first third of the new decade, Calvin's entire women's program was directed solely by Winifred Byker, a 1956 graduate. Though encumbered by facilities dating from the proverbial "dark ages," she proved more than equal to the task of further developing the teams entrusted to her.

When Byker began coaching at Calvin, the Knighties were still playing in the City Recreation's Pin-up League, in which competition was furnished by various independent teams in the area. Due in large measure to the spirited play of Louise Heeres and Dorie Zuidema, Byker's team won five of its first six games. Intercollegiate competition was furnished by Taylor University. Playing in the dormitory gym, Calvin won, 36-32, its cause having been aided by the fine play of substitutes Nita Van Dellen and Ardeth DeVries. Coach Byker's first season had been eminently successful, as her team closed its schedule with a 10-1 record and a share of the City League championship.

Byker's second year of coaching marked a decisive change in direction, as she decided to abandon City League play in favor of a schedule dominated by MIAA schools, but one that also included Ferris, Taylor, and Goshen College. Home games were shifted to the Seymour Christian School gymnasium, a new facility. The Knighties continued their excellent performance, compiling a 10-2 record their first season of exclusively intercollegiate play. Among the team's most productive offensive players were Karen Timmer, Judy Helder, Nita Van Dellen, and Eleanor Danhof.

During her third and final season as coach, Byker's squad continued to do unusually well, winning nine games while losing only one. The schedule came to a thrilling conclusion in a tough game with the Kalamazoo College Hornettes. Employing a full-court press, Calvin came back from a ten-point deficit to win by a 47-43 score. That season was the last for Eleanor Danhof, from Manhattan, Montana, who had participated in nearly every game during her four years at Calvin and who had totaled 459 points in 34 contests for a remarkable 14.6 average.

Coach Byker's final 34-4 coaching record represents a splendid accomplishment, especially since it was achieved while she taught nearly all of the women's physical education classes at Calvin. She also deserves recognition for her overall vision in advancing women's athletics at Calvin. Byker clearly helped to build a solid foundation for the program; she was a true pioneer.

In 1965 Doris Zuidema succeeded her as women's basketball coach. The Knollcrest physical education facility was now completed, so the women finally had a home court of their own. Play continued under the old rules, by which the women were restricted to a half-court game with one rover allowed to play both offense and defense. Under their new coach, Calvin's women continued to compile excellent records, going 10-2 in 1966-67, 12-3 the year following, and 14-2 in the final season of the 1960s. Yvonne Van Goor, Karen Langeland (later head coach at MSU), Carolyn Vos, Joy Mejeur, and Donna Afman led the team during those successful seasons.

1970-1979 Full Court Press

Prior to the beginning of the 1970-71 season, women's rules were finally altered, so that all players now utilized the entire court with unlimited dribble. Quite obviously, this change involved considerable adjustment for veteran team members like Vos, Joan Plantenga, Mary Monsma, and Paula Maloley. However, only one year later the "Lady Knights," as they were now known, won the state tournament and went on to the MAIAW tournament at Central Michigan University. "Little" Calvin surprised them all by advancing to the finals before withdrawing from the title game because it was to be played on Sunday (*see insert*). Zuidema's squads won state championships twice, in 1974 and 1978.

Kathy De Boer, Diane Spoelstra, and Laurie Zoodsma, a trio of exceptional athletes, played major roles in the team's early success. Their transfer to Michigan State after the 1974-75 season hurt Calvin temporarily, but Coach Zuidema made some adjustments and continued to produce top-notch teams until she left coaching basketball for field hockey. The top players during Zuidema's final year of basketball were Jan Slotsema and Kathy Nyenhuis.

Calvin's 1978-79 season was eminently successful. Coach Karla Hoesch Wolters' team fashioned a 6-0 record to win the first MIAA women's basketball championship. After her first and only season as basketball coach, Wolters

THE RIGHT DECISION

In 1971-72 the Calvin women's basketball team qualified for the Midwest MAIAW tournament by finishing as runner-up in the state tournament. Coach Doris Zuidema immediately informed the head of the tournament committee that Calvin would not play on Sunday. The event's director, not expecting Calvin to go far in the tournament, sloughed it off. However, the Calvin squad surprised everyone by reaching the finals at Central Michigan University. Coach Zuidema refused to play that final game, since it was on Sunday. Consequently, Calvin's team was designated runner-up, and the team and "Coach Z" packed up their equipment and went home.

decided to concentrate on softball and volleyball, and Esther Driesenga was appointed her successor. Driesenga coached women's basketball from 1979 until 1986.

1980-1989 Stars, Struggle, Success

For five of the seven seasons of Driesenga's coaching at Calvin, the team had modest success, finishing in the middle in final league standings. Perhaps her most outstanding player those early years was Debbie Broene, a prolific scorer who had a string of games in 1979 in which, playing against Lake Superior State, Grand Valley, the University of Michigan, and Hope, she scored 30, 30, 29, and 29 points, respectively. Two additional athletes gracing those teams were Eileen Boonstra, who set the women's single game scoring record of 40 points in 1980, and Judy Wasmer.

Yet the team did enjoy two very good seasons. In 1982-83 the Lady Knights finished their schedule with a 10-2

Debbie Broene

record and won the MIAA championship. Sharon Boeve was named league MVP for this first season of the award, a feat she duplicated in softball. For the 1984-85 season not only was the team especially competitive in every game they played, but they also compiled a fine 9-3 league record.

From 1987 until 1992 Coach Don Vroon led the women's basketball program. Vroon was glad to take up the challenge, since he thoroughly enjoyed coaching basketball. His first year was difficult, as Calvin compiled a 7-15 record, but the year following, his team won all 12 of its conference games and the MIAA championship. Julie Post was named league MVP and was one of Vroon's top players. This exceptional team was the first women's squad to participate in the post-season NCAA Division III tournament. Although his team lost to Wisconsin-LaCrosse by a score of 68-65, Vroon was honored by being named Great Lakes Regional Coach of the Year.

Although the accomplishments of Calvin's 1989 team did not match those of the previous year, the team did compile an above average 16-8 win-loss record. Two of the Knights' consistently top scorers were Sarah Ondersma and Karen Hiemstra, with Hiemstra being named to the All-MIAA first team at the close of the season.

1990-2003 Heights and Plateaus

Despite the steady play of Julie Overway and Sally Huyser, the 1990 season was mediocre. The following year saw marked improvement, however, as the Knights won 18 games while losing only eight. On a team basis, the Knights were selected to play in the NCAA Division III tournament, where they lost in the second round. Individually, two players stood out. The first was Sarah Ondersma, who concluded her career by amassing a total of 1,288 points and still today ranks near the top of the list of all-time Calvin scorers. Kim Bartman was the second standout, leading the MIAA by scoring 219 points in 12 games. The 1992 season was Vroon's last as coach of the women's team.

Sandi Struyk took over for the 1992-93 season only, but did so successfully, as Calvin became the regular season MIAA champion. The team also won the league tournament in winter 1993, the first year that tournament was held to determine which MIAA school would automatically participate in NCAA post-season play. The team lost to Wisconsin–Whitewater in the second round of the NCAA tournament. Joining Pam Wubben, who was elected to the MIAA all-league squad, was Kim Bartman, named MVP as well.

The following year, Coach Struyk was succeeded by Gregg Afman, whose resumé made him a solid choice to carry on the program. In his first year as coach, Calvin finished as co-champion with Alma College. The final regular season game determined whether the Knights would earn a share of the title. Calvin won in overtime by a score of 77-76 but then lost to Alma in the conference tournament. At the close of the season Pam Wubben was elected co-MVP.

1995 saw another tense race, with Calvin losing to Hope in the conference tournament, as Stephanie Wiers and Cheryl Essenburg were named to the All-MIAA squad. During the four years following, however, the Knights dominated the league.

In 1996 Calvin won the MIAA tournament and thus became an automatic qualifier for Division III post-season play. Though losing to Wisconsin–Eau Claire in the second round, Afman's squad compiled a fine 23-4 season record. The 1997 season saw the team duplicate its over-all 1996 win-loss record. Despite its loss to Hope in the MIAA tournament, the squad received an at-large bid on the basis of its excel-lent regular season record. After defeat-ing Baldwin-Wallace, 58-55, Calvin lost to Capitol University of Ohio, thus conclud-ing a satisfying year. Kerry Walters was Calvin's team leader and achieved all-conference honors as well. The following year, 1998, mirrored the previous season, as the Knights once again lost to Hope in the MIAA tournament, received an at-large berth, and were defeated in the second round of play, this time by Mt. Union of Ohio. Walters and Mindi Andringa led the team in scoring.

Kerry Walters

The next season, which was Afman's last as Calvin coach, saw the squad advance further in the NCAA tournament than any of its predecessors had. On its route to participation in the "Sweet Sixteen" game, the Knights first defeated Ohio Wesleyan, then heavily favored Baldwin-Wallace. Despite its loss to Wisconsin–Oshkosh in the next round, the team had compiled an excellent 24-7 season record. Both Andringa and Walters were all-conference selections. Walters, for her part, completed her stellar Calvin career as all-time scoring leader with 1,232 points, while her 616 rebounds placed her third in that category. At the end of the season Coach Afman left for Westmont College in California, having significantly raised the level of play in the Calvin women's basketball program.

Coming from Geneva College in Pennsylvania, Kim Gall succeeded Afman as coach of the Knights. Four seniors led her first Calvin team, as it won 23 games and lost only seven. Calvin finished second in the MIAA, but it upset Alma in the tournament, which led to an automatic berth in the NCAA playoffs. Once again, Calvin advanced to the "Sweet Sixteen" tournament game, defeating Lake Forest and powerful Capitol en route. The Knights won the Capi-tol game in particularly exciting fashion, as Mindi Andringa scored the deciding three-point field goal with five seconds left before the buzzer. The next tournament game, held in St. Louis, proved to be Calvin's final contest of the year, as the team lost in double overtime to Baldwin-Wallace, 76-72. That loss closed out the careers of Andringa, Robin Fennema, Jill Kreuze, and Lauren Louters. Andringa and Fennema were named to the all-league squad, while Coach Gall's team ended the season ranked ninth nationally in the final Division III poll.

Calvin's 2000-2001 team, depleted of its seniors and hav-ing to rely on many players with no collegiate experience, finished the season with a respectable 13-13 record overall, nearly defeating favored Hope in the conference tourna-ment. The following year's effort was hampered by incon-sistent play, as the Knights won half of their league games and closed the season in fourth place in the league. The 2002-2003 season saw similar struggles, as the team slipped to a tie for fifth place in the MIAA, with seniors Tricia Dyk and Emily Beard carrying most of the squad's scoring load. Although the squad's win-loss record was not outstanding, the solid individual performance of many of its members did stand out.

MEN'S BASKETBALL

1953-1959 *Winning the Tip-Off*

Calvin began its first season in the MIAA with a new coach and a team composed mostly of underclassmen. Many MIAA opponents had been on the Knights' schedules in previous years, but now, playing against them took on special meaning.

Coach Steen had prescribed a pre-season running program that resulted in a well-conditioned team. Practice took place in the cramped quarters of the "band box" gymnasium on the Franklin campus. Despite the disadvantage of having no home court all its own, the Knights performed splendidly that first year.

After two non-conference games with Aquinas and Junior College, the Knights moved through the first round of MIAA play with only one defeat, a 17-point loss to Albion. A key contest during that first half of the season was the Hope game. Every meeting of Calvin and Hope is exciting, but this one, played in the Civic Auditorium, left everyone limp, as Barney Steen's squad came out on top with a 66-65 victory.

Following a three-game, non-league interlude in which Calvin beat Ferris but lost to Aquinas and a powerful Whea-

ton team, Calvin defeated its first six league opponents in the second round of play. During this remarkable string of wins, Tony Diekema, Jim Kok, Don Vroon, and big "Sam" (Paul) Newhof, supplemented by excellent bench strength, led the way. However, Hope and Albion were right on Calvin's heels. As the season neared its close, Hope and Albion had three losses, while Calvin had been defeated just once. Although the Knights lost their final game with Hope in a high-scoring contest in the Holland Armory, Calvin surprised everyone by taking the league title during its first year of membership in the MIAA.

By winning the league championship, Calvin qualified for the NAIA (National Association of Intercollegiate Athletics) tournament. At this point, the NCAA had not yet done much for smaller colleges, and Division III did not yet exist. In the first game of the tourney, played at the Civic Auditorium, Calvin lost a tough battle to Lawrence Tech by the score of 75-59. Lawrence Tech then advanced to the playoffs in Kansas City.

The following year, Calvin picked up where it had left off, although the season proved to have its special challenges. After doubling the score on Aquinas and defeating Albion early in

TECHNICAL FOUL!

It was in a men's basketball game at Burton Gym against Adrian College. Head coach Barney Steen rarely showed displeasure with officials. At this particular game, Dave Tuuk, his assistant, was sitting next to him on the bench. Irritated by a call that had just been made, and with an official standing directly in front him, Tuuk said something like, "Open your eyes, Ref!" In response, the referee turned around and pointed at the bench, calling a technical foul. Tuuk turned around to make it look as though the words had come from the second row. And who was sitting immediately behind the bench but the gentlemanly music professor Seymour Swets!

Tom Newhof

With the starting line-up decimated by the loss of several graduating seniors, the next season saw Steen's crew win some tough games and lose others. In early season play, this inexperienced team beat Hope on the Dutchmen's home court by a 64-61 score; Steen did a masterful job of coaching by defeating a superior Hope team that would eventually tie Albion for the league championship. Tom Newhof, Ed Start, and Dave Vander Hill, along with two pesky guards, Johnnie Van Den Berg and Bill Bouman, combined to lead Calvin to do the virtually impossible. A mix of an all-court press and slow-down tactics helped the Knights win.

Although Calvin ended the season in fourth place, the year had seen some remarkable games, as the Knights split with the top teams in the league. The squad's cause was helped by the mid-year addition of Bill Morgan. After three years in the Navy, Morgan had decided to come to Calvin to pursue a pre-seminary course.

Morgan was a crowd pleaser and a showman who had developed a shoulder-fake that frequently left his defenders standing in wonderment. His slashing drives to the basket and his out-court shooting, along with his ball-handling skills, provided constant excitement for Calvin's fans. During one game, he faked a pass but kept the ball locked between his knees, to the total bewilderment of the man attempting to guard him, who didn't know where the ball had gone. This stunt proved to be a bit too much for the opposing coach to handle; after the game he commented that such play was not what the MIAA was all about.

For the 1957-58 season Calvin finally had a home court of sorts, practicing evenings and playing its home games in the new gymnasium at Grand Rapids Christian High School.

the year, the Knights lost a 67-57 game to a surprising Adrian squad led by Henry Hughes and Leon Harper. Following that loss, however, Calvin won consistently, led by Kok, Vroon, and their cohorts, and aided by the addition of 6'8" Tom Newhof, an All-City center from Grand Rapids Christian High School. In the crucial game at Adrian, lanky Jim Kok played magnificently as he and his teammates bested the Bulldogs, thus earning a co-championship. Coach Steen kept his composure, and Calvin's performance continued at a very high level.

The next season, 1955-56, was the senior year for Jim Kok, Don Vroon, and Tony Diekema. Although Calvin split with Hope, winning in Holland, 83-58, and losing at the Civic Auditorium by a score of 89-73, the team defeated Albion in a crucial homecoming game at the Civic, to take the league championship for the third successive year. Vroon, Kok, and Newhof dominated the All-Conference squad, with Don Vroon being named the league's MVP. In addition, Barney Steen was honored by being selected Coach of the Year by his Michigan NAIA colleagues.

HELP FROM HOPE

On a cold winter night back in the late 1950s, the GI bus that the Varsity Club had purchased from Army Surplus made the trip to Kalamazoo, where Calvin's JV played Western Michigan University's JV basketball team. As the bus lumbered its way homeward after the game, the driver struggled to keep the windshield from icing over. In the vicinity of Martin, Michigan, the bus finally gave out and stalled.

Unable to get it started, Coach Tuuk walked to a nearby house and rang the doorbell. When the occupants opened the door, he explained the team's predicament, indicated that he was from Calvin College, and asked if they knew anyone who could help. It so happened that these good people were the parents of Gordon Brewer, who then was the track coach at Hope College.

Mrs. Brewer called a local farmer—a handyman, she said, who could fix just about anything. This gentleman showed up in about 10 minutes, flashlight in hand, and said, "Raise the hood; we'll take a look." After checking things over, he asked, "Anyone got any chewing gum?" One of the JV players found a stick, and after he had chewed it soft, handed it to the farmer-mechanic, who used it to splice two disconnected wires. "Try it now," he suggested. Sure enough, the bus started immediately. After the team thanked the Good Samaritan profusely, the bus continued on its way and arrived back home safe and sound.

Art Kraai

Massachusetts native Don Koopman, at 6'6", joined Newhof in the front line, as Steen, knowing Newhof was about to graduate, began to re-load. Waiting in the wings were two big freshmen, Ralph Honderd and Bill Wolterstorff. The season saw two losses to a powerful Hope squad, but the Knights did well against the rest of the league, taking second place in the final standings. Calvin also went to Iowa during the holidays, winning against Augustana but losing to Central College. This was the final year of play for mainstay Ed Start, Bouman, Morgan, and Newhof, who was named All-American. Each had contributed in fine fashion to the team's success.

For the last season of the 1950s, Ralph Honderd and Bill Wolterstorff took over the front line; new at the guard position were Ed Meyering and Vern DeVries. This squad enjoyed remarkable success as it moved steadily through the league, achieving a satisfying split with Hope College along the way. Its final record was 18-2, the best of any Calvin team in history. Steen was named Coach of the Year for the second time, Honderd gained first-team all-league status as he led Calvin in scoring and rebounding, Wolterstorff made the second team, and Koopman received honorable mention.

1960-1969 *Picking Up the Pace*

As Calvin moved into the new decade, its first season saw continuing success. Although its excellent final record of 21-5 was tarnished by two losses to Hope, the Knights earned second place in the MIAA. Calvin might have had greater success still, but Ralph Honderd broke his arm in a fall during the Albion game, thus placing the burden of front-line play on Wolterstorff. However, Henry De Mots and Warren Otte filled in admirably, and Carl "Charlie" De Kuiper and Ed Meyering played well in the backcourt. The return of Len Rhoda at semester's break also strengthened the back line.

The 1960-61 season was a year to remember, as Coach Steen's finely tuned team won 20 games

1960-61 Men's Basketball. *Standing (l. to r.): Jim Kool, statistician; Jim Achterhof, manager; Don Vroon, assistant coach; Barney Steen, coach; Warren Otte; Henry De Mots; Bill Wolterstorff; Rich Rusthoven; Ralph Honderd. Kneeling: Jim Timmer, Sr.; Len Rhoda; Carl De Kuiper; Dan Bos.*

and went through the entire schedule without a loss. With the wizardry of De Kuiper in the backcourt and the scoring and rebounding of Wolterstorff and a healthy Ralph Honderd under the basket, Calvin won all of its games, though a number of them were close. A high point of the year was provided by two lopsided victories over Hope. Giving the team balance were Otte and De Mots on the front line, while Rhoda, complementing De Kuiper, played a steady game in the backcourt. The season's final game at Kalamazoo was tense and fast-paced, as Len Rhoda scored 20 points and the team made 24 of 26 free throws to remain unbeaten. The saga of this notable season will be remembered for a long time.

The following season, 1961-62, saw a bit of slippage, as Hope and Kalamazoo tied for the MIAA championship. Yet

Calvin's all-senior line-up provided fans with a great deal of excitement. In one particularly gratifying game, held during homecoming weekend, the team defeated Albion at the Civic Auditorium. With six seconds left, De Kuiper made a jump shot, thus providing Calvin with a 75-73 victory and sending a host of Calvin fans to mob their team at center court. It was a fine year for seniors Rich Rusthoven, Otte, De Mots, De Kuiper, Rhoda, and Dan Bos.

It can be difficult to sustain consistent excellence, as the 1962-63 season demonstrated. With a number of new faces in the line-up, including Ken Fletcher, Tom Vander Woude, and Jim Van Eerden in the front line, and team captain Jim Timmer in the back court, the team went through a very difficult year. The Knights suffered a long losing streak, finishing 6-15 overall and 5-7 in the MIAA, which meant a tie for fifth place in the final league standings. After the team lost a heartbreaker to Hope by a 68-66 score, its season was partially salvaged at year's end by wins over Kalamazoo, Alma, and Wheaton.

In stark contrast, the following season, to use Coach Steen's term, was "really fun." Defeating Hope twice, once by 34 points, the Knights lost only once—to Alma, their chief competitor that year. Ironically, Calvin owed its undisputed league championship to Hope, who gave Alma its second loss, while Calvin attained an 11-1 record. Jim Van Eerden broke Preston Kool's single-season record of 443 points, which dated back to 1953, and both he and Ken Fletcher made the MIAA all-conference team. An interesting sidelight of the year's activities was the fact that Glenn Van Wieren was on Hope's team, while Ed Douma played for Calvin. Some years later the two of them would serve as opposing coaches.

The 1964-65 season was the last to be played in the rented facility at Grand Rapids Christian High School. As the year progressed, Calvin developed a good record and had a solid chance of winning another championship. Steen's Knights had defeated Hope 87-64 earlier in the season; now it appeared that everything depended on whether they could win on Hope's home court. The game was tied 102-102 toward the close of the second overtime, when the referee called a foul on Kim Campbell. The Hope player made two free throws, and the game was over. The Calvin faithful judged that final call dubious and went home disheartened. Yet that difficult loss and an overall 11-11 record, including an 8-4 performance in the MIAA, could not alter the fact that Ken Fletcher, Bill Knoester, Kim Campbell, Ed Douma, and Jim Fredricks played some great basketball while at Calvin. Fletcher was once again named to the league's all-conference first team.

The following year provided two pivotal milestones in the Calvin basketball program. It was the first season the team could play in the new Knollcrest Fieldhouse, but it also marked the close of Barney Steen's career as basketball coach. Appropriately enough, it was an exciting year.

ADVENTURE IN THE SKY

In the fall of 1961, one of our pre-league opponents was Northern Michigan University, located in Marquette in the Upper Peninsula (UP). Always one for great adventures, Coach Steen arranged to have the team fly to our snowy UP destination.

We took off from Grand Rapids in a bitterly cold two-engine plane and flew to Green Bay. The next stop—so we thought—was to be Marquette. What Coach hadn't told us was that there was to be an intermediate landing in Iron Mountain, Michigan. This we discovered when the plane began to circle and the flight attendant asked us to look for a person on the ground. It was difficult, she said, to spot the unplowed runway in the UP's snowy whiteness, and this person's location would help us find it. The 12 players in the plane responded by developing an immediate case of severe anxiety, but Steen thought it was great fun.

Sure enough, one of us eventually did spy out a woman frantically waving her arms below. Near her was an arrow stamped out by footprints, indicating the direction in which we were to land. The plane set down in a huge cloud of snow, and we picked up our lone passenger. The pilot then turned our craft around and we took off, raising another cloud of snow, and flew on to our destination. Final score: 105-103, NMU.

Jim Timmer, Sr.

Calvin's team was rather "green," with many new players joining Campbell, Douma, Schrotenboer, and Fredricks. One such contributor who made his presence felt with special

COOL BREEZES

During an away basketball game at Adrian, according to Dave Tuuk and Barney Steen, Ken Fletcher was about to spring into action as a substitute. In his eagerness to play, Fletcher inadvertently pulled his basketball trunks down along with his sweat pants, creating a curious scenario. When Calvin played at Adrian the next year and Fletcher was introduced, the fans gave him a standing ovation.

Fletcher's account is a bit different; it wasn't, he thinks, all that obvious. "The way I recall it, I was sitting on the first row of the bleachers, so that you had to scrunch down to see around the scorer's table. I tried to get the warm-up off while I was sitting there. All at once I thought, 'It's cool in here.'"

However it actually went, it's still a good story.

force was Bill DeHorn, a freshman from Chicago Christian and one of Coach "Slug" Slager's graduates. A bruiser at 6'6" and a ferocious rebounder, DeHorn soon worked his way into the starting lineup.

A loss to Alma was the only blemish on Calvin's record as it went into the final game against Hope. A win would mean a championship for Calvin. It was nip and tuck most of the way, but toward game's end it was the rebounding of DeHorn and the scoring of Wes De Mots and Ed Douma that led Calvin to a 79-72 victory, causing the Knollcrest crowd to go wild. What a way for Coach Steen to conclude his coaching career—with a championship on a beautiful, new home court! Steen had coached for 13 seasons, had won 186 games while losing 90, and had led his team to six championships. As the season concluded, DeHorn won the MIAA scoring title and also was the MIAA's leading rebounder.

Beginning with 1966-67, and after serving seven years as assistant to Steen, Vroon took over varsity coaching responsibilities at Calvin. The team he inherited was not particularly fast, but it was relatively tall, with six players measuring approximately 6'4". The season proved to be bumpy, although it ended on a strong note.

Vroon's first varsity squad seemed to play in spurts, falling short in a number of close games. Early defeats by Kalamazoo and Hope seemed to unsettle the Knights. An added problem was the loss of Bill DeHorn for seven games. Coach Vroon noted that "to lose his average output of 20 points and 17 rebounds per game would be important to any team in the league."

It was due largely to the eventual return of DeHorn, who made an excellent comeback after returning to the team, that the team was able to finish strongly. The squad's final record was 10-11, including a 7-5 win-loss margin in the league. Vroon was particularly pleased with the performance of Kim Campbell, who also was named to the all-league first team, and guard Dean Douma, whose skills developed nicely during the season, as well as with Bill De-Horn's late season performance. DeHorn won second-team honors at the close of the schedule, with Hope and Kalamazoo tying for the championship.

The following season, 1967-68, met some of Vroon's expectations, but not all of them. DeHorn had transferred to Taylor, and Campbell had graduated, but Mike Phelps was a promising sophomore, and Doug Taatjes was starting to show his muscle.

Calvin began strongly, losing to Tri-State of Indiana but defeating Grand Valley and then winning the prestigious Marshall Tournament, averaging over 100 points per game in all three games. However, tough competition awaited them in the MIAA.

Early defeats by Albion (by one point) and Hope put the Knights at a great disadvantage. However, after four straight losses, the team righted itself and won five consecutive games, subduing Hope and Kalamazoo in the process. Despite the loss of Dean Douma for the season, due to a knee injury, Calvin finished second to Hope in the league standings with a 7-5 record and a 15-8 overall mark.

The 1967-68 team clearly built on the experience of the previous two years. Bill DeHorn had returned to Calvin and was joined by Ed Wiers on the front line. After successful knee surgery, Dean Douma also rejoined the team, and Mike Phelps was primed for an outstanding year. After a difficult pre-league campaign, Calvin began a 13-game winning streak, which included a victory over Hope, with Phelps, Del Willink, DeHorn, and Wiers providing key leadership. Despite Hope's 10-point defeat of Calvin in Holland, the season ended with Vroon's squad in control—and with another league championship. Phelps and Wiers were named to the All-MIAA first team, DeHorn was named to the second squad, and Douma and Taatjes received honorable mentions.

The presence of tested veterans, among them Mike Phelps, Ed Wiers, Doug Taatjes, and Del Willink, provided hope that the Knights would experience yet another stellar season in 1969-70. After losing to Wheaton in the season's opening game, Calvin defeated Hope College in overtime in Holland, with Mike Phelps scoring 54 points. The Knights then lost a tough contest to nationally ranked Ashland College and were upset by Alma at home. However, Calvin then proceeded to defeat all of their MIAA challengers, including Hope. The season's final game saw co-captains Phelps and Wiers end their careers at Calvin with an easy victory over Albion and a second-straight league championship. Both were named to the All-MIAA first team, with Phelps winning the coveted MVP award. The Albion game was also the last for steady performers Bill Van Dyke and Mike De Kuiper.

At the end of the season, and after having won consecutive MIAA championships, Vroon shocked the Calvin community and the team's fans by submitting his resignation. When asked why he was leaving the post, Vroon cited personal reasons. After expressing appreciation for the "creditable job" Vroon had done, Steen filled the vacancy by appointing assistant coach Ralph Honderd to succeed him. James Timmer was named the new assistant basketball coach.

STEEN POWER

When Calvin hosted the Michigan High School regional basketball tournament, the clamor for tickets and seats was unbelievable, especially when area Christian schools were playing. During one game Barney Steen had to solve the problem of adults sitting in a student section, and he had to do so using the public address system. In response, one woman in the crowd was heard to say to her neighbor, "Dr. Steen is the most powerful man in the Christian Reformed Church."

1970-1979 Enjoying the Heights, Enduring the Depths

Ralph Honderd, Calvin's newly appointed head coach, had good reason for feeling encouraged as he sized up his team. Doug Taatjes and Del Willink played key roles in his plans; Willink and Art Tuls, Jr., were two of the best, if not the best, passers in Calvin basketball history. Despite these gifted players, Calvin lost its first three games, to Central Michigan, Ferris, and Grand Valley. The Knights' first win in the 1970-71 season came on the road at Baldwin-Wallace on the day Ralph Honderd's son Steve was born. The victory over Baldwin-Wallace seemed to inspire the team, as it went on to become co-champions of the MIAA, sharing that honor with Olivet. Taatjes was named MVP of the MIAA that season, although the play of Willink and Tuls was also instrumental in his winning the award.

The 1971-72 season began, as was usual back then, with a game against Central Michigan. Calvin was considered the underdog, but during the first half Artie Tuls drilled four "back door" passes to his cousin Dick Frens, who went on to score easy baskets. The second half saw Central with a "box and

MULTI-TALENTED

In the early 1970s, during the "Mark Veenstra" era, Calvin's talented basketball teams traveled during Christmas vacation to several areas with strong Christian Reformed constituencies, such as Denver, Ft. Lauderdale, and Lynden (Washington). One member of the squad, Randy Wolthuis, was not only a fine athlete but also a gifted musician. On more than one occasion word got out that Randy could play both the piano and organ. As a consequence, he was asked several times to play at Sunday services. Coach Honderd was proud, the team was proud, and the churchgoers were surprised, but immensely pleased.

Today Calvin is blessed by the services of Dr. Randy Wolthuis as counselor and director of the Broene Center—and he still plays the piano expertly in campus chapel services.

one" defense, as it attempted to contain Frens. However, the rest of the team took advantage of the situation, and Calvin went on to defeat Central. That game ended an 18-year competition, as CMU felt it had too much to lose by playing in Calvin's Fieldhouse. This same Knight team went on to place second in the MIAA, finishing behind a superb Olivet squad.

After earning a co-championship with Olivet in 1972-73, Calvin went on to completely dominate the MIAA from 1973 through 1977. During those years, Mark Veenstra was the pre-eminent player not only on Calvin's team but in the entire MIAA, having been selected as the league's MVP all four years of his undergraduate athletic career (*see page 127*). Veenstra obviously could not do it alone; he was benefited during those exhilarating years by the play of a strong supporting cast of people such as Larry Vander Veen, Tom Vander Laan, Mark Hoogewind, Barry Capel, Gregg Afman, Randy Wolthuis, Kurt Vander Horst, Dwight Maliepaard, Dave Mulder, and many others.

Calvin had potential national championship teams during those years, but it was barred from post-season play by MIAA policy. The Knights never lost a game to Hope College during that span and established a 34-game winning streak against MIAA opponents. One highlight of the period was the game against Pepperdine University in 1976, the year that Pepperdine defeated UCLA in the NCAA tournament. Though defeated by a score of 92-74, Calvin played very respectably against that highly rated Division I team.

Another high point of those years was a game at Adrian played on Jaunary 31, 1976, one of the greatest contests in MIAA history. The article on page 37, printed in *Chimes*, gives an apt description of what went on.

After the 1977 season Coach Honderd indicated that he wished to be released from the demanding job of being the head coach of Calvin basketball. Don Vroon agreed to take the position once again and coached the Knights for the next seven years. Coaching a team that is under the microscope of public opinion is a daunting task. Hats off to all the coaches willing to work under this pressure!

During the next two seasons Calvin beat Hope twice. However, Albion and Alma had excellent teams during those years and effectively blocked Calvin and Hope from winning additional championships. The 1977-78 season saw Calvin lose nearly as many games as it won. The following year was more discouraging still, as Calvin, beset by ineligibility and injuries, finished league play with a 4-8 record and fifth place in the league. Tom Cooper, Mark Stacy, and the Grasmeyer brothers, Marty and Mark, carried most of the load during that burdensome year. Hope also had a difficult season, completing MIAA play with a 2-10 record. Neither Calvin nor Hope received any mention on all-conference teams. The year was an unusual chapter in Calvin basketball history.

However, the old adage that "the night is darkest just before dawn" surely proved true in this case, for 1979-80 marked a radical turnaround for Vroon's squad. Calvin and Hope were running neck and neck for much of the year, until

Veenstra scores 56 points

Knights defeat Adrian, 109-108; lead MIAA with 5-0 record

With three more victories under its belt, the men's basketball record in MIAA play now stands at 5-0. On January 24, Calvin traveled to Kalamazoo, coming away with an 88–82 victory. The following Wednesday, Calvin entertained Albion here, the result being 75–74 in the Knights' favor. Last Saturday, the result of a game was 109–108. No, the teams were not the Detroit Pistons and the Chicago Bulls. This high scoring contest was between Calvin and Adrian. The game had to go into overtime before Calvin came out the winner.

There was one unfortunate aspect to the game Calvin played against Adrian. It was the fact that the game was played at Adrian, and not many students from Calvin were able to see the game. Only those that have absolutely no interest in the game of basketball would not have been chilled and thrilled by this battle. Avid Calvin fans with weak hearts would have needed a pacemaker to survive.

The game was characterized by phenomenal shooting. Adrian shot 59 percent from the field and 86 percent from the free throw line while Calvin shot 60 percent from the field and 82 percent from the free throw line. At the end of the first half, Calvin was ahead 50–48.

The second half was also very close. With two seconds left in the game, Adrian made a basket that put them ahead 94–92. It looked like certain defeat for the Knights, but Afman took the ball out of bounds and threw it the length of the court to Veenstra. The ball deflected off of Veenstra's hands and up into the air a bit. He grabbed the ball, turned, and sunk the ball to tie the ball game and send it into overtime.

The teams started out the overtime by trading baskets. Both teams made their first four shots. But with twelve seconds left, Adrian made a basket that put them into the lead by one point. Calvin took

the ball out and moved it down the court. But it looked like defeat again when Veenstra was called for charging with seven seconds left. Adrian threw the ball in but a Calvin player was able to jar the ball loose. In the scramble, an Adrian player knocked the ball out of bounds. Thus again Calvin had just a few seconds to score, or lose.

Calvin got the ball in its forecourt. Afman threw the ball cross-court to Capel. Capel dribbled the ball towards the base line and let the ball fly with a 17 footer that went in as the buzzer sounded and gave Calvin an almost unbelievable victory.

Coach Honderd put it this way, "That was one of the best, if not the best, comebacks I've ever seen. That is the first time that twice in one game did we pull out of what was almost certain defeat." The stunned Adrian fans might have stated it differently.

Calvin **Chimes** *1976*

Hope was upset by Alma. As a result, Calvin won the league title outright, with an 11-1 record.

The Knights' last game against Olivet was a strange one. Olivet coach Gary Morrison decided to hold the ball for the entire first half, after Calvin had scored on the initial tip-off. Thus the score at halftime was 2-0. Normal play resumed in the second half, and the game ended with Calvin the victor by the score of 36-20.

After finishing in fifth place the previous year, Calvin completed its turnaround by being selected to play in the NCAA regional tournament at Wittenberg College in Springfield, Ohio. In triple overtime the Knights lost a heartbreaker to Ohio Northern, 92-90, with the Grasmeyer brothers, Mark Stacy, Don Danhoff, and Tom Montsma playing what a proud

Coach Vroon termed an "amazing game."

1980-1989 Charging Downcourt

The outcome of the 1980-81 season was both gratifying and unusually interesting. Marty Grasmeyer had graduated; joining veteran players Mark Grasmeyer, Montsma, and Danhof was Mike Kennedy, a newcomer at point guard. Calvin split its two games with Hope, but a strong Albion team made for a three-way tie in the final standings. Playoff games were held on a neutral court to determine which of the three teams would represent the MIAA in the NCAA regional. Hope drew a bye, which meant that Calvin and Albion were to face off for the first game. The night after defeating Albion by an 81-76 score, the Knights played Hope. The game was nip and tuck all the way, but Calvin defeated the Dutchmen, 71-69. Calvin did not fare well in the tournament, however, losing its first game to host college Wittenberg in Springfield, Ohio. The year had been a successful one, though, partly because Paul Ten Brink, Jerry Mastenbrook, and Richard Magsby came on strong in the closing games of the season.

Although the Knights did not do as well during the following season, they did finish second in the league with an 8-4 record. The year was a good one for Hope, as the Dutchmen defeated Calvin twice. Among Vroon's key players for the 1981-82 season were Ten Brink, Kennedy, Mike Winkle, Bruce Capel, and Larry Rosendale, with Capel being named to the All-MIAA first team.

Injuries to Tom Montsma and Randy Buist combined to hamper the Knights during the 1982-83 season, while Hope dominated the league, finishing the season with an 11-1 record. Included in those 11 wins were two victories over the Knights, who finished second with a 7-5 record. Joining Kennedy, TenBrink, and Winkle were promising sophomores Kyle Vander Brug and Ron Vander Molen.

The 1983-84 season was atypical for Calvin basketball. With an overall record of five wins and 18 losses, the team finished in last place in the MIAA. Although the Knights did not have a strong team, they were remarkably competitive in most games. The final game with Hope mirrored what had happened much of the season. Calvin was down by only one point with a minute to go, but was unable achieve a victory, losing by a score of 54-49.

In November, before the season began, Coach Vroon announced that this would be his last year of coaching basketball, since he judged that a change "would benefit both the players and the college." He submitted his resignation early, so that Calvin would have adequate time in its search for his successor. As he left the position, he noted that the combined pressures of teaching, administrative duties, and committee assignments left barely enough time for effective coaching. Since then, teaching loads in the department have been adjusted to take into account the demands of coaching.

Vroon's replacement was Ed Douma, who had been a quick, aggressive guard on Barney Steen's teams of the mid-1960s. His background included coaching at the high school level in Lowell and in Shelby, where his team won a state championship. He then moved on to a series of college and university coaching positions, first at Alma College, and then at Lake Superior State, Kent State (an NCAA Division I school), and North Carolina–Greensboro. It was from Greensboro that Douma came to Calvin in 1984.

The next 13 seasons saw a series of dog fights between Hope and Calvin for the league championship. Hope took the title the first year; after that, these rivals seemed to alternate at coming in first in the MIAA. During Douma's tenure at Calvin, his teams qualified for the NCAA tournament seven times. On occasion, both Hope and Calvin were selected for post-season play and had to face each other yet another time. Competition in these tournament games was always tough, whether the Knights were playing Hope or a team from the Ohio Conference.

During the latter half of the 1980s Douma was blessed with numerous outstanding players. First there was the tandem of Jim Schipper and Kevin Van Duyn, two talented guards who always enlivened the competition for Calvin's fans. Schipper was named league MVP in 1986. Then came the bruising combination of Dan Davis and Bill Sall, with Davis sharing league MVP honors with Matt Strong of Hope in 1988. Sall and Davis loved to play tough under the basket and constituted a high-scoring front line. Coach Douma fondly remembers how these two combined for over 60 points as Calvin defeated a Ferris State team then ranked number one in the NCAA Division II standings. During those years Calvin qualified for post-season NCAA play three times.

Needless to say, the Calvin-Hope games during that era were always thrillers. Douma remembers in particular last-second shots by Todd Hennink and Mike LeFebre that resulted in special Calvin victories along the way. Both coaches took losses to one another especially hard during those years, and fan interest on both sides was intense.

1990-1996 Soaring High: New Vistas

During the early 1990s Calvin again had many fine basketball players. One of them, Steve Honderd (Ralph's son), became a "franchise player" (*see page 127*). In three of his four seasons on the team, Calvin won the MIAA championship. The high point of the Honderd era was the 1992 season, when the Knights swept through the league 12-0 and then went on to take the NCAA Division III national championship. The tournament run included a 91-88 victory over Hope, a 69-68 win over Gustavus Adolphus, a 21-point defeat of Otterbein, a runaway victory over Jersey City, and a 62-49 championship win over the University of Rochester.

The first two games, against Hope and Gustavus Adolphus, were "nail-biters." Also notable on Calvin's part was the fact that during Final Four play, the Knights held both of their opponents to fewer than 50 points.

This 1992 national championship was the first won by any Calvin athletic team. It takes superior effort and dedication to become the best team in the nation in any division. Thus, special tribute is due to that strong 1992 team and its coach. In recognition of his superior performance, Coach Douma was voted 1992's Division III Coach of the Year.

Calvin continued to represent the MIAA in post-season play the next three years. In 1993 Calvin won the first two games of the tournament, but then lost in the sectional finals to a strong Ohio Northern team. 1993 was also the year Chris Knoester, a speedy, slashing guard, was voted league MVP. Wittenberg eliminated Calvin in the first game of both the 1994 and 1995 tournaments. The next few seasons, Calvin seemed always to be in contention for the top spot, but Hope College was the power representing the league in the NCAA tournament.

Coach Douma continues to savor the thrill he experienced in winning the national championship in 1992. As far as individual games are concerned, he remembers with particular vividness the game against Kalamazoo College in which Steve Honderd scored 61 points in an overtime struggle, thereby setting an individual, single-game scoring record that still stands.

Douma's tenure as Calvin coach came to an end at the close of the 1995-96 season. He will always be remembered by Calvin fans as a no-nonsense, astute student of the game and a master planner and strategist.

1996-2003 Millennium Mastery

After a national search, Kevin Vande Streek was named Douma's successor and assumed coaching responsibilities at Calvin in the fall of 1996. Vande Streek grew up in Waupun, Wisconsin, and graduated from Dordt College, where he played basketball. Prior to his arrival at Calvin, Vande Streek

On January 29, 1997, Calvin played Hope in the Van Andel Arena before the largest crowd in NCAA Division III history, numbering over 11,000.

coached basketball at Sioux Falls College in South Dakota.

Vande Streek's introduction to the rigors of playing against Hope was abrupt, as the Dutch won the first five games that the two teams played after his arrival. Things began to change in 1999, as Calvin tied Hope for the league championship, with both teams compiling a 10-4 record. The next three years belonged to Calvin, and in 2003 the Knights came in third.

The 2000 season, Vande Streek's fourth, was a year of outstanding achievement. Led by Aaron Winkle, a two-time MIAA MVP from Northern Michigan Christian, and featuring the excellent contributions of Holland Christian's Nate Karsten, Kalamazoo Christian's Jeremy Veenstra, and Tri-Unity Christian's Brian Foltice, Calvin went undefeated in the league and won the Division III national championship. Calvin's overall record in 2000 was a remarkable 30-2, with the two close losses coming to NAIA Division I teams Biola University and Azusa Pacific. A key, thrilling moment that season came toward the end of the Hope game, when Winkle scored a 30-foot bank shot with three seconds left in regulation time, thus forcing an overtime that resulted in a Knights win.

Calvin's successful run in the NCAA tournament began with a victory over a stubborn Franklin College (Indiana) team, when Nate Burgess made an incredible tip-in with only seconds left in the game. Calvin then hosted a sectional featuring teams from Wooster College (Ohio), Maryville College (Tennessee), and McMurray State (Texas). It was a daunting line-up, since Calvin, McMurray, and Wooster

Aaron Winkle

Jeremy Veenstra

all were rated among the top five teams nationally. Calvin soundly defeated Wooster, then completely outplayed McMurray. As a result, the Knights qualified for Final Four competition in Salem, Virginia.

Playing before a partisan Calvin crowd in the semi-final game, Vande Streek's squad nipped Franklin and Marshall (Pennsylvania), 79-77, by virtue of a last-second shot by Brian Foltice. In the finals, Calvin dominated the first half of the game against Wisconsin–Eau Claire, leading by 16 points at the break. The second half was a different story, but the

Knights hung on to defeat them by two points, thus winning Calvin's second Division III national championship. Winkle was named National Player of the Year, and Vande Streek was accorded Coach of the Year honors.

The years immediately following, though marked by solid success, were in a sense almost anti-climactic. Calvin did win the league championship in 2001 and 2002, with Jeremy Veenstra forming the backbone of the team. Although the 2003 season belonged to Hope and Albion, Calvin's five decades of MIAA basketball had been eminently successful.

MEN'S CROSS COUNTRY

1953-1959 Runners (Almost) Ready

A prerequisite to Calvin's joining the MIAA was the addition of one more sport, since it was league policy that all members had to participate in at least six of the seven it sponsored. Since Calvin's program consisted of only five sports, it was necessary to generate a sixth. The only realistic choice was cross country.

Dave Tuuk and Barney Steen, the latter Calvin's newly appointed director of athletics, took on the challenge of assembling a cross country team for the first year of competition. And a challenge it was. Prior to 1953, Calvin had had no program for training distance runners, and cross country involved a four-mile race. To supplement Pete Steen and Morrie Turbergen, the two experienced distance runners who turned out for the team, Barney Steen decreed that all basketball candidates, like it or not, had to be involved in pre-season conditioning—in this case, training with the cross country team. The hope was that those who showed promise of cardiovascular endurance might well become members of the cross country squad. The strategy actually was somewhat successful: two aspirants to the basketball team, Don Vroon and Bob Kooistra, showed real promise. Thus was born Calvin's first cross country team.

Home meets during the 1953 season were held at Indian Trails Golf Course. Contrary to expectations, that first team enjoyed remarkable success, defeating four of the league's eight teams and finishing a solid fourth in the standings. Hope and Albion shared a co-championship that first year and gave Calvin's coaches a good picture of what lay ahead, if they wished to build a championship team.

Dave Tuuk took over sole coaching responsibilities for the 1954 season, during which Calvin, led by Tubergen, Vroon, and Don Greenfield, jumped up a notch to take third place in league standings. Tuuk's squad maintained that place the following year as well, with Pete Steen and Bob Korthuis leading the way. Albion, with its abundance of talented runners, continued to be the top team in the league.

During the 1956 season, Calvin lost some of the impetus it had built up over the previous three years. Tuuk's front runner, Bob Korthuis, did well, but the team lacked experienced runners to back him up. The result was a fifth-place finish. 1956 did see an important development in Calvin's program, however—the establishment of a four-mile, contin-

ROLLING HOME

Part of Barney Steen's training regimen for basketball players during the early years of Calvin's MIAA membership consisted of the requirement that we run with the cross country team, presumably to get in shape. Although I ran reluctantly, I also must have run just a bit too well, for on one occasion, when the cross country squad was short of runners, I was called up to run with the team at an away meet at Albion.

Halfway through the race, while I was grimly contemplating how I could avoid this torture in the future, I lost my way. As I looked around, I saw a course "checker" sitting not far away in a pickup truck. I asked him if I could ride in the back of his truck to the finish line. He agreed, and I finished the course sitting in the back of a pickup.

As I rejoined the team, I got some curious looks from Steen and his squad. But the result of it all was delightfully predictable. Never again was I "invited" to run at a competitive cross country meet!

Anthony J. Diekema

Calvin runners at the start of the 1958 MIAA championship meet held at Hillsdale College.

uous home course on the recently acquired Knollcrest Farm, today the site of Calvin's beautiful campus. Bert deVries, a member of Calvin's first team to run at Knollcrest, remembers the boost given to the program by the new home course.

The next season Calvin regained the momentum established by its first three teams. Two bright freshman prospects joined the team: Barry Koops, of Rehoboth, New Mexico, and Jim DeBie, who had run at Grand Rapids Christian High School. Both were talented runners, and deVries remembers

clearly how their attitude soon began to permeate the entire squad. The 1957 season culminated with Calvin's hosting the league championship meet on a cold, rainy day with a muddy track. With DeBie and Koops finishing second and third, Calvin regained the third-place standing it had enjoyed in 1954 and 1955. After that meet, Albion's coach sensed that his team's domination of the league was soon to be threatened, remarking that the rest of the league should "look out for Calvin in the next few years."

That prediction proved to be on the mark, as the Knights convincingly led the MIAA for the next two years, winning their first championship in 1958 and repeating in 1959. Joining Koops and DeBie as Calvin's top runners were Nels Miedema from Hudsonville, Al Bierling from Denver, and Ron Van Mersbergen from Bellflower, California. In 1959 Calvin actually shut out six of its seven league opponents, winning each time by a score of 15-50. DeVries clearly recalls how the turnabout was a product of both Tuuk's fine coaching and the influence of this small influx of talented runners, who taught the rest of their teammates that there was no substitute for off-season training. No longer did team members show up in September, muttering, "I have to get in shape." The new attitude paid immediate dividends, and the foundation was laid for Calvin's rich cross country tradition. Those gains were to be measured not only in terms of the team's success, however. DeVries remembers with gratitude the caring attitude of Coach Tuuk and the feeling of camaraderie that made participation in those early teams both a privilege and a rewarding experience.

1960-1969 Sprinting Out, Ending Fast

The autumn of 1960 saw a continuation of the excellence marking the previous three seasons. Not only did DeBie and Koops return for their senior year, but Ray Hommes, a gifted freshman runner from New Jersey, also joined the team. The squad's overall strength resulted in an undefeated league season in which Calvin won all of its dual meets by a perfect score, 15-50—a feat never before achieved in league history. Jim DeBie had a fine year, taking first place in many meets, while Barry Koops struggled with injuries. However, in the conference meet, Koops came through with a remarkable performance, taking the blue ribbon.

The Knights capped their fantastic year of success by their performance at the NCAA College Division meet in Wheaton, Illinois, finishing seventh on the Chicago Country Club course. Koops earned 10th place and DeBie came in 15th, resulting in All-American status for both runners. Calvin's eighth season in the league clearly had been a banner year.

SOFT-SELL RECRUITING

The summer of 1957, after graduating from high school, I was clerking at Van's Hardware in Lynden, Washington. One afternoon a young Calvin alum came in, looking for me. "I'm Pete Steen," he said. "I hear you're going to Calvin. You ought to run cross country."

At that time the longest distance run in high school competition in my home state of New Mexico was the mile. I had never seen a cross country race and had only a hazy idea of what one might look like. But I was flattered that this sophisticated Easterner would know I even existed, much less that he would come to see me. In his low-key way, he made a vivid impression.

When I arrived in Grand Rapids, I found Coach Tuuk's office on the first floor of the dorm even before signing up for classes. "Four miles," he said, "and just like golf, low score wins." I thought I could probably run four miles and signed my name on Dave Tuuk's clipboard.

Pete Steen pointed me down a fork in the road, and, as Robert Frost says, "That has made all the difference."

J. Barry Koops

The next three seasons, 1961 through 1963, saw similar success. Koops and DeBie had graduated, but their places were taken by a dedicated group of new runners: Fred Kamper, Al Zietsma, Lou Mensonides, Jack Bannink, and Tom Broersma. Hommes led the team during these years, as Calvin again defeated all league opponents and won its fourth, fifth, and sixth consecutive league titles. The team also gave strong performances in the NCAA Championships, placing ninth in 1962 and sixth in 1963.

All good things must come to an end, even record-setting winning streaks of 39 dual-meet victories. In the first MIAA meet of the 1964 season Albion defeated Calvin and went on to win the league championship, with Calvin taking second place. However, this Calvin team gave an excellent account of itself in the NCAA Championships, placing 10th out of the 23 select teams entered.

During the next four years, 1965 to 1968, the Knights' performance was somewhat uneven. They earned a third-place finish in 1965, sagged to fourth in 1966, then rebounded to second in 1967, with Jim Admiraal leading his teammates. In 1968 Bill Lautenbach led the team in a rebuilding year, as Albion and Adrian produced particularly strong squads.

1969, on the other hand, was a remarkable season for Calvin. The team had lost close meets to both Adrian and Alma during the regular season, and finished that part of their schedule in third place. In the conference meet at Adrian, however, Calvin surprised everyone by taking first place, while Alma came in second and Albion third. Consequently, Calvin tied with Alma for the co-championship. Hats off to the Calvin runners who showed so much heart: Dave Kingma (4th place), Bill Lautenbach (5th), Ken Key (6th), Nick Koster (12th), Tom Boogaart (15th), Joe Day (16th), and Ron Nydam (18th). Thus the 1960s began with championships and closed with a co-championship, while the team experienced some ups and downs during the middle years of the decade.

1970-1979 *Uphill Most of the Way*

During the early 1970s it seemed as though the bottom had dropped out of Calvin's cross country program. Numbers were down, and those who did participate were inexperienced. Calvin's fate in the conference meet in the fall of 1970 was symbolic of the way the entire year had gone. Because coaches misread the schedule, Calvin arrived at the site of the meet too late to do normal warm-ups, and as a result, dropped back to a sixth-place finish in the league. The only bright spot for the Knights was Randy Veltkamp, a talented freshman from Timothy Christian in Chicago. 1971 saw yet

another sixth-place finish for Calvin, and marked perhaps the lowest point in Calvin's cross country program since its inception.

In 1972 the race distance was increased from four to five miles, which posed a major adjustment for Calvin's young, inexperienced runners. Thus it was no surprise that the squad once again ended the season in sixth place. Only in 1974 did the situation begin to improve, when Calvin tied for fourth place and compiled a 4-2 dual-meet record. The Knights maintained that position in 1975, when Marvin Rus and Tim Zwier led the team to another fourth-place finish. The 1976 team was strengthened by four promising freshmen: Phil Vannette, twins Larry and Garry Quakkelaar, and Justin Wilson. With Tim Zwier, they helped propel Calvin to the runner-up position behind Hope in the league standings.

Despite the success of the previous season, 1977 began with dimmed hope, as a number of leading runners did not return to the team. However, once again there were four freshmen who joined Marvin Rus to constitute a strong squad: Doug Diekema, Rich Poppe, Mark Wisse, and Mark Hannink. The season's first dual meet was held at Hope, the defending league champion, with Calvin a decided underdog. In one of the great dual-meet victories in the history of the program, Calvin surprised Hope, winning by a score of 28-30. Though Hope dominated all opponents for the rest of the season and won the conference race as well, the Knights were pleased with their co-championship.

Even though Diekema continued as one of the top runners in the league, Calvin could do no better than third place in 1978. However, 1979 was another story. Once again, an influx of new runners, among them John Brink, Kurt Mast, Mike Verkaik, and Chris Vander Baan, strengthened the team significantly. Running with Diekema and Poppe, these newcomers helped Calvin to a 25-30 defeat of Hope and to another co-championship, with Hope edging Calvin in the conference meet. After a difficult beginning in the early 1970s, Calvin had won its way back to solid respectability by the decade's end.

1980-1989 Running Tough

As the new decade began, Calvin's team continued to show consistent strength. Doug Diekema, now a senior, was joined in 1980 by Brink, Mast, and several additional runners who helped provide team depth. A high point of the season was Calvin's showing in the prestigious Carthage (Wisconsin) Invitational, where the team took first place, competing against larger universities such as Northwestern, Marquette, and DePaul, as well as a number of state schools in Wisconsin. Diekema finished in second place, only five seconds behind the leader from Marquette University, while Brink took fourth place and Mast finished sixth.

During the early 1980s, Hope continued to be Calvin's chief league rival. Although the Knights defeated the Dutchmen 23-33 in their dual meet and finished 6-0 in that segment of league competition, Hope edged Calvin by a scant eight points in the conference meet. The result was another co-championship for Calvin. The team ended its season very successfully, placing second in the NCAA Division III regional meet and a very respectable eighth in nationals.

1981 saw a similar scenario, with Calvin defeating Hope in a close dual contest, but losing to the Hope squad in the conference meet. The result was a fourth consecutive co-championship for Calvin. The next year, however, was another story, with Calvin winning the conference meet as well as going undefeated during the dual-meet season. After slipping to a third-place tie with Albion in 1983, Calvin repeated its performances of 1980 and 1981, sharing yet another co-championship with Hope, the fifth since 1977. Although Calvin had many fine runners during these early years of the new decade, the remarkable achievements of John Brink, who finished second in the NCAA national meet and was a three-time All-American, clearly stand out.

The 1985 season was to be Dave Tuuk's 33rd and final year as cross country coach. Although Calvin's team was very young, it achieved a very satisfying second-place league finish. Hope was still, in a sense, "king of the course," but that was soon to change, as Brian Diemer was appointed

Tuuk's successor. Tuuk himself knew that, in his own words, "to be succeeded by an Olympian would pay great dividends for the Calvin cross country program in the future."

Diemer proved to be the right person to succeed Dave Tuuk and to build on the solid tradition Tuuk had helped establish during his long tenure. To begin with, he had impeccable running credentials, which included fine success as a steeplechaser on the University of Michigan track and field team and membership on three American Olympic teams. In 1984, just two years before becoming coach at Calvin, he had won the bronze medal in the Olympic steeplechase. In 1992 he was elected captain of the entire American Olympic contingent. In addition, he had won an impressive array of Big Ten, national, and international awards. Complementing those achievements was his wholehearted agreement with Calvin's Reformed, Christian educational mission, including its philosophy of athletics. All in all, he proved to be a perfect fit for the position at Calvin.

John Brink

From the very beginning, Diemer coached in tandem with Al Hoekstra, who had himself been a distance runner while at Calvin. Working together, the two of them have had eminent success as coaches, confidantes, and spiritual leaders of Calvin's cross country athletes.

The first year of the new regime, 1986, saw solid success, with Calvin once again placing second in the MIAA final standings. Rick Admiraal and Roosevelt Lee were two prominent team leaders that first season. However, the Calvin program blossomed fully one year later, in 1987, when the Knights won the league championship and placed Rick Admiraal, John Lumkes, Pat McNamara, and Adam Suarez on the all-conference squad. That championship was to be the first of 17, extending to 2003, and established the current dominance of Calvin as a cross country power.

The final two years of the decade saw the continuation of the program's notable success and the emergence of several new standout runners to complement Lumkes and Suarez—among them, Jeff Avery, Dwayne Masselink, Mike Miedema, Thad Karnehm, and Dave Sydow. Both Lumkes and Karnehm later ran in the American Olympic trials. Thinking back on those first years as coach, Diemer remembers with particular gratitude the leadership of Rick Admiraal and John Lumkes.

1990-2003 Cruising the Hills: Unbroken Excellence

During the next 14 years, Calvin not only continued to dominate the league, but also established itself as a national power in NCAA Division III cross country circles. The team qualified repeatedly for the NCAA championship meet, and with the exception of the 1991 and 1992 seasons, placed each year in the top 10 nationally. The last five years, 1999-2003, have seen particularly remarkable success on the national level, with Calvin achieving one fourth-place finish, two second-place finishes, and two national championships, the first in 2000 and the second in 2003.

Such success would not have been possible without a host of gifted, dedicated athletes. Not all of those who contributed meaningfully to the continuation of Calvin's rich cross country tradition won national honors, but Diemer and Hoekstra continue to respect the key roles they, too, played on various teams.

Yet a team doesn't win league or national championships without a full quota of front runners. Since 1991 Calvin has placed 73 team members on the All-MIAA squad; during that span 15 Calvin runners were named MIAA Most Valuable

Runners. Ray Van Arragon won the award three times and Geoff Van Dragt twice. Justin Pfruender, Dan Hoekstra, Paul Petersen, and Joel Klooster won All-American honors in leading Calvin to its first national championship in 2000, but they represent only five of a total of some 28 All-American finishes achieved by Calvin cross country athletes since 1991.

Diemer and Hoekstra consider Calvin's 2003 cross country team to be "perhaps the greatest athletic team Calvin has ever had." On the way to winning

Dan Hoekstra

a second national championship, the team swept the top six places in the MIAA, the top five in the NCAA regional meet, and in the championship meet finished with the second best total score in NCAA Division III history, as it outpaced its nearest competitor by 80 points. Winning an unprecedented six All-American designations were Hendrik Kok, Matt Edwards, Tim Avery, Dave Haagsma, Tim Finnegan, and Kris Koster. Brian Paff, the runner whom Diemer calls the "glue" of the championship team, didn't even run in nationals, willingly giving that opportunity to a teammate. Diemer stresses that it is that kind of attitude, repeated many times over by many athletes, that ultimately forms the foundation of Calvin's remarkable program.

WOMEN'S CROSS COUNTRY

1980-1989 Through the Valley and Toward the Heights

It was in 1980 that the MIAA introduced a cross country program for women. Since only Albion, Calvin, and Hope fielded teams, cross country was initially classified a club sport. Dave Tuuk, the men's cross country coach, was in charge of this new group of runners.

The initial year of competition went well, when one considers that not all team members had even had running experience in high school. Calvin won its dual meet with Albion, lost to Hope, and placed well down the list in meets with much larger schools. In the "conference meet," such as it was, Laura Vroon, Calvin's top runner, took first place, while Ruth Prins came in third, Deb Dahnke fifth, Linda Vroon seventh, and Esther Wilting eighth. Thus Calvin's team took home the club championship trophy in its first year of competing in the sport.

The next year, in 1981, the MIAA upgraded the status of women's cross country and made it a championship sport. During this season Alma and Albion tied for the top spot, while Calvin came in third and Hope fourth. Laura Vroon placed second in the league meet, Tara DeVries came in 12th, and Ruth Prins finished 13th.

Despite outstanding performances by Laura Vroon, Calvin could do no better the following season than share a tie for third place with Hope, finishing behind Alma and Albion. Vroon once again ran second to Lisa Thocher of Alma; Ruth Prins and Leslie Wheaton were the only other Calvin runners to place in the top 15.

1983 was, in some respects, a notable year for Calvin's young program, mostly because Laura Vroon enjoyed exceptional success.

Laura Vroon

Vroon, now a senior, capped her career by winning first-place honors in the MIAA championship meet and being voted league MVP. The year was remarkable also because for the first time, Calvin entered a team in the NCAA Great Lakes Regional meet. True to form, Vroon once again ran a stellar race to capture first place with a time of 18:07 for the 5,000-meter course. Her victory entitled her to compete as an individual in the national meet in Fredonia, New York. Although she did not place high, she ran a good race and had the thrill of running her last race wearing a Calvin uniform in a national meet.

During the next two years Esther Driesenga, a Calvin staff member, assumed coaching responsibilities. Leslie Wheaton led the team in 1984, as Calvin tied Hope for second place. 1985 saw a repeat second-place finish, with Hope winning the championship.

With the appointment of Nancy Meyer as coach in 1986, Calvin's fledgling program gradually established itself as top-rate. However, success did not come overnight. Coach Meyer didn't even have five runners for the first meet of the season, so her team went to the dorms and enlisted the services of four raw recruits in order to be able to simply field a full team and thus to compete. Despite that difficult beginning, Calvin still managed to finish third in the league.

The 1987 team doubled in size to 13 and once again finished third in the MIAA, behind Hope and Alma, although Calvin's Debbie Vander Steen took first place in the conference meet. The impetus that had begun to build in 1987 continued in 1988, as the team's size grew to 19 members. Although Calvin lost to Hope in a dual meet, the Knights defeated the Dutch at the league championships on a very rainy, muddy day, thus earning a co-championship. Vander Steen, Shelley DeWys, Kim Talbot, and Shari Vander Horn took four of the eight available All-MIAA spots. The team finished third in the NCAA Regionals, where Deb Vander Steen advanced on an individual basis to the national meet in St. Louis, becoming the first female runner since Laura Vroon to achieve that feat.

Among the new faces on the 1989 team were Heidi Lanning and Jenny Rozema, and the team on the whole was stronger than that of 1988. However, Calvin's experience running against Hope mirrored that of the previous year, as the team lost to the Dutch in a dual meet, but defeated them in the conference championships. Deb Vander Steen continued with her strong performances and was elected league MVP. The year was notable also because Calvin won its first NCAA regional title and thus qualified for the nationals at Augustana College, where they placed 11th among the 14 participating teams. By the close of the decade, Calvin's women's cross country program definitely had established itself. However, greater things were still to come.

1990-2003 Running Strong

1990 was supposed to be a rebuilding year for Calvin, since seven of the squad's 14 runners were new to running on the college level. Despite modest expectations, however, the team took its first league championship outright, won the NCAA regional meet, and advanced to nationals. Although Calvin came in 13th in a field of 14, the year had been surprisingly successful.

A great crop of freshman runners, including Laura Erffmeyer, Amy Rideout, and Renea Bluekamp, helped strengthen the team in 1991, as the Knights became MIAA champions and NCAA regional victors, and finished in eighth place nationally. Calvin's reputation as a cross country power had begun to attract an excellent array of serious runners. Coach Meyer also got valuable help when men's cross country co-coach Al Hoekstra agreed to take on added responsibility as assistant for the women's program.

Great senior leadership, maturing sophomores, a fine freshman addition (Amy Kuipers), and keen competition from an improved Hope team pushed Calvin to a new and higher level of performance in 1992. The team, running with the confidence it had developed over the course of the entire season, won a fourth consecutive NCAA regional championship and was runner-up in nationals, despite very inclement weather. Erffmeyer and Kuipers were named All-Americans, while Heidi Lanning, running the race of her life, barely missed out on that honor.

If Coach Meyer wondered whether the 1992 season was a fluke, the 1993 season proved her wrong. Betsy Haverkamp, a future national champion in track, joined the team, and was instrumental in helping Renea Bluekamp regain her competitive fire. League and regional championships were followed by another second-place performance at the national meet. Had illness and injury not intervened, Calvin might well have won the NCAA Division III championship outright.

The 1994 season fully matched the success of the previous year, with Betsy Haverkamp, Amy Kuipers, and Amy Rideout leading the team to the league and regional title. Once again, Calvin finished second to Cortland State in the NCAA championships, with Kuipers, Rideout, and Haverkamp winning All-American status.

The 1995 squad, joined by Andrea Clark, Sarah Gibson, and Kristie DeYoung, struggled with injuries, but was nevertheless able to repeat its run to league and regional championships and managed a fourth-place finish in the national meet. Amy Kuipers achieved All-American status for the fourth year, only the second woman in NCAA history to earn this distinction, and was rewarded with a standing ovation from the crowd at the national meet.

1996 proved that Calvin's successful run was by no means over, as the team, led by Haverkamp, Clark, and newcomer Lisa Timmer, once again achieved a fourth-place finish in the NCAA nationals, with Haverkamp and Timmer winning All-American honors—Betsy Haverkamp, like Amy Kuipers the year before, for the fourth time.

The 1997 season, marred by injuries and inclement weather, did not witness the success of the previous year, despite the addition of several talented new runners. The team continued its tradition of winning the MIAA and NCAA regional meets, but it dropped to ninth place at nationals. Despite what would have been considered notable success by most teams, Calvin's team and coach were disappointed.

That very disappointment, however, helped fuel the 1998 season, which proved to be a magnificent year for the Knights.

THE RIGHT STUFF

Though only a freshman, Lisa Timmer became an All-American in cross country in 1996. In 1997 she and her teammates once again competed in the NCAA Division III championship meet, which was held this time in Boston's Franklin Park under horrific weather conditions. Timmer ran very well, but with only 300 meters to go, her legs gave out in the deep mud, and she was forced to nearly crawl to the finish line, completing the race far back in the pack.

Though disappointed by her showing in Boston, Timmer and her teammates resolved to do better the following year. And they did. In 1998 the women's team won the national championship, and Timmer earned All-American honors for a second time. The following year, Timmer and Amy Mizzone led their team to yet another national championship. By the time she graduated from Calvin, Lisa had won three All-American plaques, and her team had won two national championships. Boston's mud clearly had not broken her spirit.

The season did not begin in promising fashion, as five Calvin runners, men and women, had to be hospitalized with heat stroke. All five recovered, however, and from that point on, the women met every goal they had set for themselves, including the league, NCAA regional, and national championship. A number of factors contributed to these fine achievements. One, according to Coach Meyer, was a very active team prayer life. Another was the consistently excellent performance of the squad's leaders and the confidence that runners such as Amy Mizzone, Timmer, Kuipers, Clark, and Rashel Bayes developed. Yet another was the rolling course on which the national meet was held. As a bonus to an already wonderful season, Meyer was named National Coach of the Year.

Most of Calvin's lead runners returned for the 1999 season, and although the season was not as flawless as that of the year before, the team nevertheless repeated its league, regional, and national championships, a truly stunning feat. Three Calvin runners won All-American status: Kuipers, Timmer, and Mizzone. With back-to-back national championships, Calvin's program had gained national prominence.

The 2000 season was not without its high points. Calvin won the league championship, and Sarah Gritter was named conference MVP. After those league victories, however, the team appeared to lose some of its focus, struggling to win regionals and then finishing a disappointing 14th in the national meet, which was held on a cold, snowy day.

The following year's team was blessed with a full supply of gifted runners, among them Erinn Boot, Lindsay Carrier, and Rachel Baber, a transfer from Dordt College. As had nearly become a habit, Calvin easily won the league and regional championships and approached the national meet at Augustana with high hopes. Those hopes were met with only partial fulfillment, however. Whereas in the previous year cold temperatures and snow had helped defeat Calvin, this time it was scorching heat. Nevertheless, Calvin finished in a very creditable sixth place.

Prospects for an excellent year were high as the 2002 season began. Baber, Calvin's lead runner, was back, as were senior runners Jessie Lair, Sarah Hastings, and Tami Vermeulen. Despite an unfortunate spate of injuries, the team performed well, winning its 15th consecutive league title and 13th regional championship. Another successful season ended with a fifth-place finish in the national championships.

The year 2003 had its high points, but it also brought a measure of disappointment. Gifted freshman additions to the team were hampered by injuries and by a lack of confidence. Despite these handicaps, Calvin won the MIAA Championship. However, for the first time in 14 tries, it failed to win the regional title, coming in second. In the national meet the team struggled, finishing in 15th place.

Success, however, is relative. Although the 2003 season was less fulfilling than in previous years, winning the MIAA for the 16th straight year and competing on the Division III stage underscored a legacy of excellence in women's cross country.

Amy Kuipers

WOMEN'S FIELD HOCKEY

1965-1969 Promising Beginnings for "Hockey on Grass"

In the mid-1960s, as the new campus was being developed, the women's athletic program launched a new project. Staff member Nita Vander Berg was given the challenge of beginning a women's field hockey club.

There was a certain amount of student interest in this sport, but for the most part, those who wished to participate had very little experience, since few high schools sending women to Calvin sponsored field hockey teams. It took a good deal of patience and teaching skill to introduce interested students to the fundamentals of the game.

Field hockey is not for the timid or faint of heart. Found primarily on the college or university level, it is a fast-moving team sport played on a level grass field, much as soccer is. Each of the eleven players on the team wields a stick with a curved end; only the flat side of the stick may be used to play the ball. Field hockey demands endurance, skill handling the stick, speed, teamwork, agility, and hustle. Action is continuous, and, like soccer, the game allows no time outs.

After assembling a squad and working on the basics of the game, Coach Vander Berg scheduled games with those MIAA schools that already had field hockey programs. In 1968 Calvin became a part of a loosely organized league composed of teams representing these schools. The squad also played teams from larger universities such as Michigan State, the University of Michigan, Western Michigan, Central Michigan, and Northern Michigan. A highlight of those early seasons was a 3-1 victory over Central Michigan, in which Edie Tameling and Marcia Voortman scored for Calvin.

In 1969 Karen Timmer replaced Vander Berg as coach. Under both coaches, Calvin's women were known during these first five years for their consistently tough, competitive play.

1970-1979 Attaining Goals

Annelies Knoppers coached the team from 1970 through 1972, while Lori Hageman, who had just completed four years as a player at Calvin, took over the squad for the following three years. From 1973 until 1977 Albion, Kalamazoo, Adrian, and Olivet were dominant in the fledgling league. Though neither Hope nor Calvin was particularly successful during that span, their rivalry continued unabated, each team winning approximately half of the games they played against each other.

RIDING THE "BIKE BUS"

One of the most notable trips the field hockey team took involved participation in a national tournament at Slippery Rock State College in Pennsylvania. Since college policy demanded that all students attend their regular schedule of classes, Calvin's team was not able to leave until late Friday afternoon. Rather than have her squad sleep sitting on the hard seats of a regular bus, Coach Doris Zuidema decided to travel by the "Bike Bus," the vehicle equipped with bunks that was used when Calvin sponsored summer bike trips. After a full night of bumpy travel and intermittent sleep, the team arrived at the tournament site Saturday morning, just a couple hours before their game began.

A significant turnabout took place in 1977, when Doris Zuidema, who wanted a change from coaching basketball, succeeded Hageman. Largely as a result of her enthusiasm, quick grasp of the new sport, and coaching expertise, Zuidema's teams enjoyed early and consistent success. Already in 1979, Calvin, led by the superb play of Julie Besteman, won the SMAIW State Tournament and went on to the national tournament at Princeton.

During this period, Calvin's women were members of the AIAW and SMAIW, which, like the men's NCAA, controlled regional and national competition. At the turn of the decade, the MIAA assimilated women into its structure in terms of governance, scheduling, eligibility, awards, and the like.

1980-1990 Continuing Success, but a Bittersweet Ending

The 1981 season saw a remarkable achievement for Calvin's program. The Knights, playing a double round-robin sched-

ule, went 12-0 while winning the MIAA championship, the only time this feat occurred in league field hockey history.

The years immediately following were marked by consistent parity, with no single team dominating competition, but Calvin did win the MIAA title in both 1985 and 1986. The 1986 season, in fact, was outstanding. After winning the state championship and playing in the regional tournament, Coach Zuidema's squad became the first MIAA team to participate in NCAA national tournament play. That same year, Lisa Van Dellen was the league scoring champion and Lisa Reeder was voted league MVP, an honor she earned four successive years.

Calvin continued to do well during the remaining few years of formal MIAA competition, winning three additional championships, for a total of six during the life of the program. However, scheduling became increasingly difficult, since ultimately only four teams remained: Calvin, Hope, Adrian, and Kalamazoo. As a result, simply to keep the sport alive, it became necessary to schedule games with schools in Indiana and Kentucky, which necessitated long, time-consuming road trips. Deb Bakker coached Calvin for the final two years it fielded a team; in 1990 field hockey was discontinued as an MIAA sport. Its lifespan had been short but nevertheless meaningful for the many Calvin women who had participated in the program.

MEN'S GOLF

1953-1959 Increased Expectations and Floating Sand Traps

Men's golf has been a part of Calvin's intercollegiate athletics program since 1933-34, when Coach A. H. Muyskens led the first team. However, with Calvin's entry into the MIAA in 1953, pressures and expectations for the team increased.

During most of the 1950s, economics professor John Vanden Berg served as coach, although he was temporarily replaced at two junctures by chemistry professor "Doc" DeVries and biology professor Martin Karsten. An intramural tournament was generally held in the fall in order to identify potential members for the coming spring's team. The season consisted of dual meets and a final tournament, with both counting toward the MIAA championship.

According to Vanden Berg, the team was quite competitive during the first half of the decade, due in large measure to the fine play of two Irish brothers, Bill and Tom O'Hara, in the number one and number two positions. After graduation the O'Hara brothers left the Grand Rapids area, but they returned each year to participate in the alumni tournament,

in which they played against John Vanden Berg and John Vander Henst, the latter another excellent golfer in the teams of the early 1950s. These twosomes generally competed for top honors in the tourney.

Back in the 1950s, the team usually practiced at the Ridgemoor Country Club at the corner of Breton and Burton. Practice was somewhat sporadic and often done on an individual basis, following Coach Vanden Berg's suggestion that "you fellas oughta get out there and play a bit." Golfers had to pay for their own rounds, equipment, and golf balls. Winter practice, such as it was, was occasionally held in the old Franklin dormitory gym. Those indoor sessions must have been curious experiences.

Greenridge Country Club in northwest Grand Rapids was Calvin's home course during most of the decade, although the team also played at Blythefield, Cascade, and Kent Country Clubs. The MIAA league tournament was usually hosted by Kalamazoo College at the Kalamazoo Country Club.

Judging by *Prism* accounts of the late 1950s, the team suffered its share of mild frustration. One *Prism* story describes the sand traps during a given match as "running around the course in a desperate effort to place themselves underneath the lofted sphere." Wins during those seasons were not common occurrences, but trips to Lawrence Tech and a season-ending picnic attended also by wives and girl-friends helped contribute to an atmosphere of fun.

The decade of the 1950s concluded with a winless 1959 season, the *Prism* tersely noting that "Professor John Vanden Berg fared better in local politics than his golf team did in its competition."

1960-1969 Consistently in the Rough

The men's golf teams of the 1960s did not generally do well. For most of the decade, Barney Steen served as coach, although speech professor Lester DeKoster also led the Knights early on.

Dave Tuls

In the 1950s it had been Bill and Tom O'Hara who starred for Calvin; for several years in the 1960s it was Paul and Dave Tuls, graduates of Holland Christian High School who played the first and second positions and scored consistently in the upper 70s. An indicator of both Paul Tuls' personal ability and the team's persistent struggles was the fact that he was the only Calvin all-conference player selected during the entire 10-year span.

The decade did have its highlights, although they may not have been numerous. Knight wins included numerous victories over Hope College, including a lopsided 14-1 win at the American Legion Course in Holland in 1967. Another signal moment occurred in 1966, when Calvin defeated perennial league champion Alma by a score of 9½–5½. Coach Steen's "WOW!!" written on the result sheet of that match tells it all.

PULL THAT PIN!

The closest Calvin came to the league championship in men's golf was in 1965. According to the report printed in *Chimes*, except for a tough loss to Albion, 8½–7½, near the season's end, the Knights would have won at least an MIAA co-championship. A penalty stroke assessed a Calvin player for tapping in a putt without pulling the pin out of the cup made the difference in the crucial Albion match. So near, yet so far . . .

1970-1979 More of the Rough

As had been the case during the previous ten years, the new decade was characterized by the excellent play of individuals such as Lloyd Dozeman, one of Steen's top golfers, who was medalist in 1970 with 150 strokes in two rounds. Yet the team as such did not experience significant success. Representing Calvin as all-conference selections during these years were Don and Bruce Vande Vusse and Ken Huizenga, all three of whom did their best to carry their squads.

Despite the rather consistent mediocrity of Calvin's teams, the decade was nevertheless notable, largely because of a number of changes it brought in league policy and practice. In 1972 golf became a fall sport for the first time, and in 1975 the conference instituted stroke play instead of match play. In 1978 the MIAA championship was awarded for the first time on the basis of total strokes for the entire league season. Replacing dual matches that year were seven-team jamborees hosted by member colleges.

Records of matches played during the 1970s also disclose an oddity—a substitution rule. According to this rule coaches were allowed to substitute one player for another at any time during the match. Thus on September 27, 1973, for example, Coach Steen substituted Stan Hoksbergen for Greg

Van Stee after the first nine holes, in which Van Stee had shot a 38. Hoksbergen then scored a 39 on the second round, making for a total score of 77. Needless to say, this rule has long since been abandoned.

1981-1989 Back on the Fairway

Referring to the 1980 men's golf team, the 1981 *Prism* noted, "Perhaps you saw them—those faithful few who diligently swing the club. They comprised the men's golf team under the coaching of Barney Steen. Low ranking within the league plagued Calvin all season." It seemed that nothing had changed. However, better things were in store.

As the years passed, gradual change set in. In 1981 Jim Timmer, Sr. replaced Steen as coach, and it was in the mid- to later 1980s that the "diligent swinging" of Calvin golfers began to pay off. With a place to practice daily, first at the Grand Rapids Golf Club, then at the Forest Hills Golf Club, Timmer's squad progressed to four consecutive second-place league finishes from 1986 to 1989. Ever since the 1950s, the team had seen the strong play of individual golfers, but now it was combined with steadily increasing depth. The results were gratifying.

Foremost among the individual golfers who stood out during these years were all-conference performers Steve Kraai in the early 1980s, Howard and Dan Vroon in the mid-1980s, and Steve Ritsema, who received the honor four times between 1986 and 1989.

1990-2003 Chipping Away . . .

During this 13-year span Calvin golfers finished in second place in the MIAA twice. In 1994 Jeff Timmer and Bruce Langerak were keys to the Knights' runner-up performance. Timmer's 1994 performance was no fluke. During his under-graduate career as a Calvin golfer, his average score for all rounds played was a remarkable 76.3, a feat no other golfer in the history of the program has equaled. Although their play fell just short of Timmer's, two additional golfers of the 1990s should also be mentioned: Bryan Hoekstra, who was

medalist at two of the jamborees in 1999, when Calvin also came in second in the league, and Mark Van Stee, who was voted All-MIAA all four years of his career as a Knight.

Jim Timmer, Sr. retired as golf coach in 2003 after faithfully and ably serving the college for over three decades.

Jeff Timmer

WOMEN'S GOLF

1991-2003 Teeing Off

In 1991, after coaching the field hockey team for 13 years, Doris Zuidema initiated Calvin's women's golf program. The squad's first season was remarkably successful, as it finished in second place in the league. Team leader that first year was Kim Bartman, who had been a state champion golfer for Calvin Christian High School. At the close of the season she was named to the All-MIAA first team, having compiled a 92.0 stroke average. Bartman is currently the only Calvin female golfer in the history of the program to receive that first-team honor.

The Lady Knights continued to play respectable golf for the next few years. The team finished in fifth place in 1992, with Jody Heeringa leading the squad with a 95.5 stroke average and earning second-team honors on the All-MIAA roster. The following year, Coach Zuidema's squad moved up one notch, to fourth place, in final league standings, with Heeringa-Heilman once again team leader and recipient of a second-team All-MIAA slot.

The next season, 1994, saw Calvin duplicate its fourth-place finish of the previous year. Joining Heeringa-Heilman

on the All-MIAA second team was Rebecca Van Drunen. 1995 was the final year Zuidema coached the team. During this season the team inched up to third place in league standings, with Van Drunen and Sally Van Dokkenburg winning second-team All-MIAA honors.

Ed Douma served as interim coach in 1996, when the team placed fifth in the league. He was replaced by Ralph Honderd in 1997, when the squad could not consistently field enough players to constitute a full team, although Kara Hugen placed fifth in individual league standings. In 1998 the team, led once again by the play of Hugen, finished in eighth place, and in 1999 it dropped to ninth place. In both 2000 and 2001 the Knights finished in seventh place, although they came in third in the MIAA championships in 2001. That third-place conclusion to the season was a portent of better things to come.

Jerry Bergsma succeeded Honderd in 2002, as his nearly all-freshman team, except for sophomore Dawn Svenkeson, moved up three spots to fourth place in the league—Calvin's best finish in seven years. Annie Huizenga's 93.2 stroke average was the fourth best in Calvin women's golf history, as she gained second-team all-league honors. Although Bergsma's squad slipped to fifth place by a narrow margin in 2003, its season had several highlights. Calvin placed third in both the Aquinas Invitational and the Hope-Calvin Invitational and played exceptionally well in the MIAA championships. Annie Huizenga's single-season record of 91.0 surpassed the record Kim Bartman had set back in 1991 and won her second-team All-MIAA honors. Huizenga was the first to win such

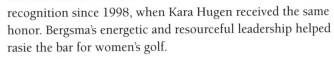

Kim Bartman

Annie Huizenga

recognition since 1998, when Kara Hugen received the same honor. Bergsma's energetic and resourceful leadership helped rasie the bar for women's golf.

WOMEN'S SOCCER

1988-2003 *On the Ball*

In the early 1980s women's soccer was played on the club level at Calvin, but in 1988 it became a varsity sport, and in 1989, an MIAA sport.

The 1988 season went well, as Calvin compiled a 9-5 record while playing a number of MIAA schools, as well as a few Division I institutions such as Central Michigan, Michigan State, Notre Dame, and Western Michigan. Coach Dan Ackerman's squad was led by the play of Cheri Drukker and Missy Van Heukelem.

With the introduction of soccer as an MIAA sport in 1989, Mike Petrusma became coach, a position he held until 1994. Calvin barely missed becoming league champion that first year of play, losing only in overtime to Kalamazoo. Gretchen Toxopeus joined Drukker and Van Heukelum in leading the Knights to a fine 11-2-1 season. Drukker and Toxopeus were rewarded by being named to the All-MIAA first team. That runner-up finish to Kalamazoo was the first in a series of four, which ended only in 1993.

In 1990 Calvin's MIAA record was 5-1, while its total season brought 11 wins and four losses, one of which was to Michigan State and another to Notre Dame. At the conclusion of the year, Michelle Swierenga joined Toxopeus as an all-league first-team designee.

The following year's schedule was played within a new MIAA format, as member schools had both home and away games with each league opponent. Calvin's overall record of 11-6 included a 9-3 MIAA performance. That same season saw Missy Van Heukelem complete her soccer career as the first Calvin player to score more than 100 career points. She was joined by Swierenga as an All-MIAA first-team selection.

In the 1992 season Calvin established a new record for total season victories, winning 15 games but losing only four. Two of the matches Calvin dropped were, once again, to powerful Kalamazoo. However, the year did bring a new single-season scoring record, as Julie DeGraaf finished with 54 points. Goalkeeper Becky Reimink, who recorded a remarkable total of 10 shutouts for the Knights, and Kristin Penzotti, another outstanding performer, became first-team MIAA honorees for the year.

Although in 1993 Calvin defeated Kalamazoo for the first league loss ever suffered by the Hornets, the squad slipped to third place for the season. The following year saw a return to the runner-up position, as Penzotti set two records. Not only did she score a total of 152 points during her years at Calvin, but she also was the first Knight to be named league MVP. Together with Julie DeGraaf, she earned first-team all-MIAA honors.

Deb Bakker faced a daunting rebuilding task as she assumed coaching responsibilities in 1995. However, she capably met the challenge. Despite the loss of five starters and seven seniors, her squad enjoyed a splendid season, attaining Calvin's first league championship with a sterling 11-0-1 record, while winning an additional six non-league games and losing none. Freshman Tara Dyk set new single-season records in goals (27) and total points scored (64). Nearly half of Calvin's starters placed on the all-league team. The squad experienced a bit of a disappointment at year's end when, despite its impressive season, it did not receive an invitation to the NCAA Division III tournament.

The Knights repeated as league champion the next two years, compiling a 10-0-1 record in 1996 and an 11-0-1 total in 1997. In 1997 Calvin was ranked sixth in the Division III national poll and was selected to be host for the Great Lakes Regional. After receiving a first-round bye and then defeating Denison, the team's remarkable run came to an end. The season featured a 19-win record, however, and Tara Dyk was named the MIAA's MVP, the second Calvin player to be given this honor. Dyk also set another single-season scoring record in goals and total points. Once again, nearly half of Calvin's starters were accorded either first- or second-team All-MIAA honors.

Although Calvin did not win the league championship in 1998, the season was in its own way satisfying, as the team finished with a 15-7 win-loss record and a tie for second

Tara Dyk

Tricia Dyk

place in the MIAA. Among those 15 victories were wins over nationally ranked William Smith and Wheaton. Despite its failure to take the MIAA title, the team was invited to play in the NCAA Division III tournament, losing in the first round to Denison by a 1-0 score. Two of Bakker's players distinguished themselves in stellar fashion in this final season of their careers. Tara Dyk finished as all-time Calvin leader in goals, assists, and points, while Cara Jansen was named second-team GTE Academic All-American for the second straight year. Both players also achieved the distinction of being named to the All-MIAA first team for the fourth consecutive year.

Despite fielding a youthful squad made up exclusively of underclassmen, the 1999 team performed very well, finishing the season in second place in the league. Freshman Tricia Dyk took over her sister's role as scoring leader, registering 17 goals for the year. Dyk continued her fine performance in 2000, scoring 12 goals, four of which were game winners, as Calvin once again finished second in the league. Among the highlights of the season was Dana Haan's last-minute goal against Kalamazoo, which enabled the Knights to defeat the Hornets for the first time since 1997. Dyk, Haan, and April Phelps were honored by being selected for the first-team All-MIAA squad.

Under newly appointed coach Mark Recker, the team continued its solid play in 2001, achieving a 15-5 record overall and a league record of 11-3. Three of the squad's five losses were to nationally ranked teams. Dyk continued to excel in league play, leading the MIAA in both goals scored and points.

The 2002 season was characterized by a number of close games, as four of Calvin's six losses were by one goal. Despite a third-place finish in the league, nearly half of Calvin's squad was named to the All-MIAA first team. Dyk finished her career by being named to the Great Lakes all-region team as well.

Calvin came close to winning the league championship in 2003, but found itself in second place at season's end. The team concluded its MIAA schedule with a fine 10-2-2 record, as Sarah Weesies was elected league MVP.

All in all, Calvin's relatively young program in women's soccer has been notable for both outstanding individual play and consistent team success during the first 15 years of its existence. Its future can only be termed promising.

MEN'S SOCCER

Preamble: Calvin Soccer Before MIAA Competition

Soccer at Calvin began in 1957, when a group of seminarians and college students formed a club and played pick-up games in the spring and fall. Soccer as an actual varsity sport was instituted in 1959, when Calvin's team joined the Midwest Collegiate Soccer League, playing opponents such as Michigan State, Purdue, Indiana, Wheaton, and Goshen. Roel Bykerk, professor of psychology, coached the 1959 team; for the 1960 season he was joined by Tony Brouwer, professor of economics. The majority of players back then came from a Dutch background. These early teams, coached after 1961 by Marvin Zuidema, enjoyed a measure of notable success against tough competition. The 1962 team actually tied Michigan State for the Eastern Division Championship of the league. Calvin's goalie that year, Casey Ter Haar, won All-American honors.

It soon became evident, however, that the Knights could not continue to compete against large universities offering soccer scholarships. As a result, Calvin participated in 1966 in the formation of a new league, the Michigan-Illinois-Indiana (MII) Soccer Conference, whose member institutions were liberal arts colleges. Although the team's efforts did not produce spectacular results during its four years in the new conference, it was able to compete successfully. Among Calvin's more gifted soccer players were the sons of missionary families like the Reckers, who had learned the game in the host country in which they had grown up, as well as talented products of newly established high school soccer programs in various regions of the United States. Calvin's "Canadian Connection" was also strong during this time and furnished its full quota of solid athletes.

After the 1969 season, the MII was no longer operative; both Calvin and Hope dropped out to take part in MIAA play. Although the league had existed only four years, it played an important transitional role in the history of Calvin's soccer program.

The 1970s and the Onset of MIAA Competition

In 1970 the MIAA made men's soccer a championship sport. Participating squads that first year were Albion, Calvin, Hope, and Kalamazoo. Olivet joined in 1975, Alma entered league play a year later, and Adrian began its participation in 1981.

Calvin's first decade of MIAA soccer saw sterling success. Led by Coach Zuidema, the Knights either won or shared the championship in 1970, 1971, 1973 through 1976, and 1979, compiling a 156-17-20 league record those first 10 years. The 1976, 1977 and 1978 seasons stood out as being particularly successful, with Calvin going undefeated in league play over a three-year stretch, while also doing well in non-league competition. The Knights' roster was composed of a host of excellent players, far too many to list in this context. Some 21 team members won All-MIAA first-team honors, while MIAA Most Valuable Player awards went to Don Buchholz ('71), Tom Van Tongeren ('72 and '74), Jim Johnson ('73), Roger King ('76), and Mark Recker ('78 and '79). (Please see the appendix for a complete listing of all players who won All-MIAA status.)

Many of these excellent athletes had been on high school teams whose coaches had previously played for Calvin. However, players with an international background also contributed significantly to the team's success. Two of them, Jim Johnson and George Saa, were from Liberia, while Tom Van Tongeren and Mark Recker had learned the game in Nigeria.

A number of soccer players in the 1970s also played on other Calvin teams. Among them was Mark Stacy, who was a starting guard on the basketball team and a starting back on the soccer team. Stacy did not take up soccer until he

was challenged by his roommates to do so prior to his junior year. Despite the late start, he developed into an all-conference player by the time he graduated.

Many of the Calvin teams playing in this decade probably could have enjoyed success in post-season NCAA championship play. However, MIAA policy forbade member schools from entering that tournament. League policy-makers felt such involvement could threaten the balance of academics and athletics.

However, the Knights did participate in a number of tournaments during the regular season. The 1973 team participated in the Far West Soccer Classic, held in California, advancing as far as the tournament finals, when it lost to Westmont College. Tournaments played in Ohio, Illinois, and Indiana against teams such as Wheaton, Wooster, DePauw, Wabash, and Ohio Wesleyan also were favorite events during these years.

1977 saw the soccer squad's first trip to Europe, where the Calvin team learned firsthand that Europeans can really play the game. That initial trip abroad was threatened with financial disaster, when it was feared that a travel agency had mishandled team funds. With help from a U.S. Consulate, however, the situation was ironed out, and the team returned home with many good memories.

End-of-season letters Zuidema sent his players often stressed his concept of "educational athletics." They also stressed that, while soccer was to center on fun and competition, it also provided constant opportunities to further develop Christian attitudes and values.

1980-1989 Continuing the Legacy

Calvin's teams in the 1980s picked up where their Knight predecessors in the 1970s had left off. During the new decade, the Knights won four league championships and never finished lower than second place. Calvin's overall MIAA record for those 10 years was 92-12-14.

The 1980 season was particularly exciting and satisfying. Calvin had finished second to Hope during league play, los-

FALSE ALARM

A team prank just prior to the crucial Hope game in 1980 unsettled Coach Zuidema mightily. Only hours before the game was to begin, several players got together and "forged" a note from goalie Brett Van Tol, in which Van Tol announced he had decided to quit the team. After an anxious hour of searching for his presumably retiring goalie, Zuidema was relieved to discover the origin of the note, as well as to learn of Van Tol's full intention to play that day.

ing the championship by virtue of a tie. Despite its runner-up performance, however, and by virtue of its 3-1 defeat of Hope, Calvin was selected over league champion Hope to receive a controversial invitation to the NCAA tournament. Calvin thus became the first MIAA soccer team to participate in post-season NCAA play, which had been sanctioned by the MIAA in 1976. And the Knights made the most of this opportunity.

Calvin first defeated DePauw by a score of 4-3. The team followed this win with a 1-0 upset of highly favored Ohio Wesleyan, thus earning a spot in the national quarterfinals. However, on a cold, icy November day on their home field, the Knights fell to the team from Scranton (Pennsylvania) by virtue of a first-half penalty kick. Despite this difficult loss, it had been an exhilarating tournament run characterized by excellent play and experiences not soon to be forgotten.

Doug DeSmit

The 1980 team was led on offense by Doug DeSmit, Ron Nyenhuis, and George Saa. With nine shutouts during the season, the team's defense held opponents to 0.94 goals per game against mark. Together with Saa, Scott Hamstra, who had helped anchor the team's stellar defense, was named a member of the All-MIAA first team.

The 1981 season built on the success of the year before, with the Knights winning the MIAA title outright with an 11-1-0 record and being invited once again to participate in NCAA championship play. Although Calvin could not repeat the previous year's NCAA upset of Ohio Wesleyan, losing this time by a score of 4-2, the season was nonetheless noteworthy. Doug DeSmit, Keith Saagman, John Wilks, and Mark Schlenker earned first-team league honors, while DeSmit earned the MIAA's Most Valuable Player award.

The 1982 season was a major disappointment. Although Calvin won the MIAA championship with a 10-1-1 league record, Hope College, with a 9-2-1 record, was selected to participate in the NCAA tournament. In a sense, the controversial invitation to Hope in 1982 was a mirror image of

Calvin's disputed selection in 1980. Despite this disappointment, the season had been outstanding, with Calvin placing four players on the All-MIAA first team and DeSmit once again earning MVP honors.

Calvin finished in second place in 1983. However, it was a year in which Doug DeSmit won special honors. In addition to being named league MVP for the third straight year, he also became Calvin's second soccer All-American, following Casey Ter Haar, who had won that honor in the 1970s. DeSmit's career total of 128 points continues to stand as an individual league record.

1984 saw Calvin regain the MIAA championship. In the summer of that year, soccer players also had another opportunity to go to Europe. The season ended with a first-round 2-1 loss in the NCAA tournament, the victor being Ohio Wesleyan once again.

Calvin finished second to Kalamazoo the next two years, but in 1987 the Knights once again won the league championship with an outstanding 11-0-1 record, with David Fasold winning league MVP honors. The season was

TIMEOUT IN SOCCER?!

The rule book makes it very clear: There are no timeouts in soccer. But one time that rule was broken by Coach Zuidema, and without penalty.

In a typically intense, physical game at Hope, Zuidema feared that open hostilities were about to break out. As one of the Calvin players took a swing at a member of Hope's team, Zuidema quickly and loudly called "time-out." The official was so taken aback that he blew his whistle, actually stopped play, and allowed both teams to huddle.

Zuidema maintains to this day that he actually talked only about sportsmanship, not about tactics, during this unprecedented time-out. We shall choose to believe him. In any case, fair play was more in evidence after the interruption than it had been before.

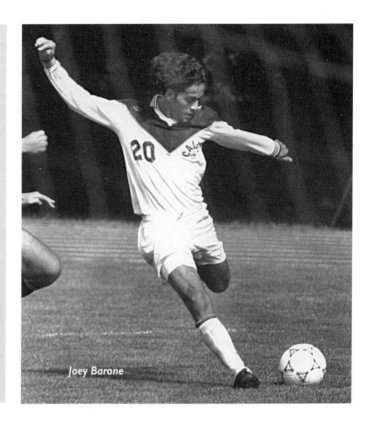
Joey Barone

also notable for a non-league victory: for the first time in 29 tries, the Knights were able to defeat Wheaton. The two teams had played to a tie a number of times, but 1987 saw Calvin's first outright victory.

In both 1988 and 1989 Kalamazoo had excellent soccer squads that finished with undefeated league records. Yet the Calvin teams of those years had some outstanding young players who would help set the tone for the 1990s. Fans still talk about the ball-handling and shooting skills of Joey Barone, the wonderful game sense of Ed Wilgenburg, and the fantastic saves of the Veenhuis brothers, both goalies par excellence.

All in all, Calvin soccer was once again highly successful in the 1980s. However, the Kalamazoo Hornets and Hope Flying Dutchmen always made the league race interesting, with Kalamazoo, under Coach Hardy Fuchs, winning four championships and Hope taking the league title once.

1990-2003 Books and Goals

Prior to the new decade, the educational perspectives that underlie athletics at Calvin were usually understood and accepted by Calvin athletes. The need for this perspective probably was more important in the 1990s than ever before. First, due to an increased emphasis on sports in American culture, athletes were confronted daily with the challenge of blending academic work and intercollegiate athletics. The growth of recruitment and the snowball effect of more and more athletic involvement made it difficult for all Calvin athletes to maintain a healthy balance. And second, the 1990s were characterized by increased parity in MIAA soccer competition. The league saw the blossoming of more and more quality players, and Kalamazoo, Hope, and Alma fielded particularly strong teams. Consequently, winning became more difficult for Calvin, and team unity and Christian humility were frequently tested.

The 1990s began on a promising note, however. Joey Barone, Ed Wilgenburg, and Todd Veenhuis were back and formed an excellent team nucleus. In many ways, the season did meet expectations. Calvin went 11-1-0 in MIAA play, tying Kalamazoo for the championship. The co-championship was achieved when, toward the game's end, the Knights eked out a 3-2 victory in a classic game against the Hornets. Joey Barone, Ed Wilgenburg, Chris Hughes, and Todd Veenhuis were named to the All-MIAA first team. Despite the team's 14-3-1 record overall, it was not invited to NCAA post-season play, a disappointment that forced the Knights to think long and hard about the basic meaning of athletic involvement.

The 1991 squad emulated the achievements of the year before by once again winning an MIAA co-championship. In addition, because of its excellent 19-2-1 overall record, the team won the right to participate in the NCAA tournament. After defeating Kenyon College in first-round play, Calvin lost to Ohio Wesleyan in a night contest in Delaware, Ohio.

This game marked the end of the brilliant careers of Joey Barone and Todd Veenhuis. True to form, Veenhuis played a marvelous game in goal in the loss to Ohio Wesleyan, making one save that can only be classified, in Zuidema's terms, as "an impossible stop." Barone, for his part, set six school records that still stand. Coach Zuidema considers this group to be "one of the best Calvin soccer teams ever assembled," in terms of both character and athletic success.

The following six seasons saw the establishment of parity in the MIAA. From the onset of league play in 1970 through 1991, Calvin had always finished in first or second place in MIAA standings. That situation was now to change.

In 1992 and the year following, Calvin finished third; from 1994 to 1997 the Knights could do no better than a fourth-place finish, and the 1997 squad, which was involved in many close games, was the first in Calvin history that failed to win more games than it lost. During this six-year period, Calvin nonetheless placed nine players on All-MIAA first-team rosters. Zuidema credits not only his players but also various assistants and JV coaches for the invaluable role they played in Calvin's program, among them Mark Van Harn, Tom Wybenga, Chris Riker, Wayne Huizinga, Chris Hughes, Daryl Michael, and Erwin van Elst.

After a long and successful career, Zuidema retired as coach at the end of the 1997 season. During his tenure, Calvin enjoyed a fine success ratio, with a .613 winning percentage. In 1998 the National Soccer Coaches Athletic Association provided a fitting climax to his career by granting him the prestigious Bill Jeffrey Award for his contributions to the promotion of soccer in the United States. In 1998 the MIAA honored him by establishing the Dr. Marvin Zuidema Award, given annually to a senior MIAA player who exhibits excellent soccer skills, academic achievement, leadership, and ethical character. Although he gave up his coaching duties, Zuidema did retain his position as NCAA Division III chairperson for the National Soccer Coaches Athletic Association.

David Ver Merris, who had been a very successful soccer coach at Western Michigan Christian High School, and whose teams had won several state championships, became head coach at Calvin in 1998. During the four years of his tenure, Calvin's program enjoyed solid success. After a third-place, 8-5-1 league record in 1998, the Knights won a co-championship in 1999. In 2000 they finished in second place in the league, and the year following they again came in third. During Ver Merris' term as coach, several players were honored by being selected as members of All-MIAA teams: Marcus Byeman, Peter Knoester, Todd Folkerts, Jake Wisner, and Jason DeJonge.

After Ver Merris left Calvin in 2002 to become principal at Western Michigan Christian High School, former player and JV coach Chris Hughes was named head coach. Under his direction, Calvin's fine tradition continued. In 2002 the Knights came in third in the league, and in 2003 they shared the championship with Hope College. During those two years Joel Veldhouse, Joel Vande Kopple, and Kurt Visker won All-MIAA honors, and Visker was named the league MVP. Veldhouse won an additional honor when he was named to the first team Academic All-American squad. The grand tradition of Calvin soccer continues to hold solid promise.

WOMEN'S SOFTBALL

The Years Before 1979: Struggles and Strikeouts

Softball is a game that people of all ages enjoy playing. Thus it is no surprise that as far back as the late 1940s, Calvin women moved to establish it as an intercollegiate sport. Until the early 1970s, however, a combination of factors worked against that effort, among them a lack of facilities, the absence of league affiliation, and the priorities of a busy Calvin physical education staff.

However, the situation began to change not long after the decade of the 1970s began, when Nita Vander Berg, a member of the P.E. staff, was encouraged to start a club team. Early games played at the Christian Reformed Recreation Center helped generate the impetus to establish softball as a varsity sport. In 1975, after two years of additional club play under Coach Kathie Pott, the sport was elevated to varsity status, and Lori Hageman, a newcomer on Calvin's P.E. staff, was commissioned to lead the effort.

Hageman, ably assisted by Evan Heerema, coached the Knights for the next four years. During that span, Calvin did well against other MIAA teams also with fledgling programs, but fared less well against larger schools such as Michigan State, Western Michigan, and Central Michigan. However, despite seasons characterized by mediocre win-loss records, the Calvin women were learning the essentials of the sport.

Among the pitchers who stood out during those initial years were Nancy Meyer and Lori Plaisier. Karla Helmholdt, a particularly talented catcher and hitter, also distinguished herself in those years. Reports of those early games also mention the hitting exploits of players such as Bonnie Knaack, Deb DeHaan, Mary Hamelink, Jan Slotsema, and Kathy Nyenhuis.

Among the team's losses during those years, one nightmarish game in particular stands out in Coach Hageman's memory. Playing without solid pitchers and on a field without fences, Calvin's inexperienced women lost to Michigan State by a score of 24-0. Although Hageman had understandable fears that the game might never end, her players survived intact, and when, at year's end, they were asked for the impressions left by the season, they stressed the invigorating challenge provided by competition and the joy of becoming better acquainted with their teammates. Win, lose, or draw, the experience had been enjoyable.

The closing years of the 1970s showed noticeable progress in the development of Calvin's program. In 1977 the

Calvin softball teams always gave their all.

championships. All in all, from 1979 through 1984 the squad won 53 league games while losing only six, a record little short of amazing.

A great deal of the credit for Calvin's success was due to the coaching of Wolters, who not only brought great enthusiasm

squad placed a solid fourth in the state tournament, and wins over teams from smaller colleges boosted the team's confidence. However, the Knights did not yet play on a par with teams such as Michigan State, Western Michigan, and Grand Valley. Former players reading this account may remember a particularly unsettling double header against Oakland University, when Oakland's players resorted to overt mockery of Calvin's squad. Justice was served late in the second game, however, when Coach Hageman's team came back from a five-run deficit to defeat their chagrined tormenters.

The following year was somewhat disappointing, but happier days were soon to come.

1979-1989 Clearing the Bases

Karla Hoesch Wolters coached Calvin softball for the next eight years and did so in superb fashion. During her first season, 1979, bad spring weather was a potential deterrent to success, but Wolters alleviated the problem by scheduling carefully planned indoor workouts. That strategy paid off, as Calvin won the league championship that first year, finishing with a 9-1 record. After sharing the title with Olivet the following year, the Knights proceeded to four outright MIAA

to the program, but also worked hard to refine all facets of the team's play. It should also be noted that her teams' excellence was developed despite significant improvement in the programs of other MIAA colleges.

Of course, even the best coaching will not produce winning teams without the contributions of outstanding athletes. Pitchers Sharon Boeve and Laura Vroon, also known for their hitting, helped the Calvin cause enormously during those years. Boeve was named the league MVP in 1983 and 1984. Not only did both Vroon and Boeve compile perfect 5-0 records in 1984, but Boeve also led the league in hitting with a .471 average, and Vroon came in third, batting

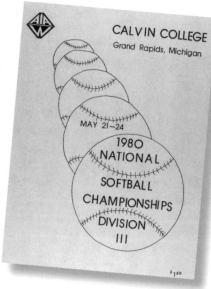

CALVIN COLLEGE
Grand Rapids, Michigan

MAY 21-24

1980 NATIONAL SOFTBALL CHAMPIONSHIPS DIVISION III

Cover of the program for the national championships hosted by Calvin.

.394. The MIAA has seldom, if ever, seen a tandem of such outstanding ability on one team.

Vroon and Boeve did not do it alone. Their success was immeasurably enhanced by the catching skills of Janna Ter Molen. They were also supported by the play of teammates such as Leslee Shaw, who won the league batting title in 1981, and four-year players Deb Bakker in the outfield and Deb Dykstra at third base. Another component in Calvin's success was the constant chatter of Pam Lancaster, dubbed "Team Spirit" by her fellow players.

The Knights' tradition of great pitching continued after Vroon and Boeve graduated. In 1987 Jessica Schrier did an outstanding job and was named league MVP. That year was to be the Wolters' last as Calvin coach, as at the end of the season she returned to her alma mater, Hope College.

Wolters' notable success at Calvin had not been restricted to MIAA play. As early as 1981 Calvin hosted and participated in the National AIAW Softball Tournament. Playing against teams of exceptional caliber, the Knights did not fare well that first year. Among the remarkable athletes participating in that tournament was Kathy Arendson of Chico State, a native of Holland and graduate of Holland Christian High School who later starred on the U.S. Olympic team, eventually becoming one of the world's premier women pitchers. The year following, however, Wolters' team did significantly better, placing fourth in the nation, an achievement she terms one of the high points of her 13 years on the Calvin coaching staff.

Waiting in the wings to replace her former coach in 1988 was Janna Ter Molen, whose four-year experience as catcher had helped prepare her in unique ways to take over Wolters' position. It is commonly known that catchers develop a kind of intuition that later makes them successful coaches; Ter Molen was no exception. Her first year of coaching met with immediate success, as Calvin, led by league MVP Anne Boshoven, won the MIAA title. Laurie Hiemstra, batting an amazing .632 for the season, became MVP in 1989, as the Knights not only finished first in the league but also took the regional championship, which qualified them for national finals play. Two wins over Cali-

fornia–San Diego placed Calvin in softball's "Final Four," where losses to Buena Vista of Iowa and New Jersey's Trenton State ended the team's remarkable run. The decade of the 1980s had been eminently satisfying for Calvin softball.

1990-2003 Stars and Strikes

Though runner-up in regular-season league play in 1990, Calvin qualified for regional NCAA competition by eliminating favored Adrian in the MIAA tournament. After advancing by virtue of two wins over Milliken, the team traveled to New Jersey for the national tournament. The Knights defeated Allegheny in the first round, but then headed home after losses to Trenton State and Eastern Connecticut. Kristi Klaasen and Laurie Hiemstra made special contributions to the team's success, the former as a pitcher and at second base, the latter as an outfielder-pitcher.

With the departure of Coach Ter Molen for graduate school, the softball program struggled somewhat. The next four years saw a succession of four coaches. The resulting disruption did not make the team's task easier.

Kristi Klaasen, who had enjoyed a stellar career as a player, coached the squad in 1992, as Calvin compiled a 6-4 record in league play and earned fourth place in the standings. Julie Overway was the regular catcher, Sima Pandya anchored the infield, and Barb Manwell was a solid performer in the outfield. Pitching duties were shared by Shelly Woertink and Shan Gray.

In 1993 Bill Vander Vennen, a former Calvin baseball player, pinch-hit as coach. The result of the season's play was another fourth-place finish in the MIAA and an overall 6-17 finish. The 1994 squad was coached by Kari and Karla Kunnen, who had played championship softball for the University of Michigan. Under their leadership, the team compiled an 18-14 season record, which constituted a significant improvement from the previous year. Pitcher Holly Ondersma, with an 1.82 ERA, ranked third among MIAA pitchers; among her back-ups was Sara DenHartigh, a promising first-year player from California.

The Kunnen sisters continued to assist in the Calvin program the following year, 1995, but Deb Bakker took over chief coaching responsibilities for both the 1995 and 1996 seasons. The 1995 season saw the appearance of Shauna Koolhaas from Escondido, California, one of the most notable players in the history of Calvin softball. Not only did Kohlhaas have a tantalizing rise ball, but she also showed incredible endurance, on occasion pitching both ends of a doubleheader. In one remarkable week she actually won seven games. Her contributions were pivotal in 1996, as Calvin tied Hope for the league championship with a 10-2 record. After eliminating the Hope squad in the NCAA regional, Calvin lost to Chapman by a 6-0 score.

When Amber Warners, a member of the P.E. staff, became coach in 1997, she inherited a rejuvenated program and was successful in sustaining the momentum the squad had built up for yet another year. During her first season as softball coach, the Knights tied for first place in the final MIAA standings, won the league tournament, and captured the team's first Central Region NCAA title since 1990. Although the squad was stymied in national-level play, both Koolhaas and Melanie Harriff were named All-Americans. In addition, they shared league MVP honors. Attesting to the excellence of Calvin's program was the fact that its 1997 appearance in the national tournament was its ninth.

Shauna Koolhaas continued her excellent play in the 1998 season and was joined on the all-league first team by Rhonda Volkers and Marissa Van Koevering. In 1999 Calvin finished second in the MIAA tournament and third in final league standings. Both Sara Plasman and Volkers placed on the All-MIAA first squad. 2000 saw the team break even in regular season league play, although its overall record was 12-19.

After a losing season in 2001, Calvin, led by the play of Laurel Sands, came back to compile a 20-17 record in 2002, finishing fourth in the league. The team's record in the MIAA in 2003 was 10-4, while it won 24 games and lost 13 overall. Jeanne Cole and Rachelle Heyboer placed on the all-league first team, and Heyboer was named Most Valuable Defensive Player. The Knights continue to field solid teams and now look forward to the future with confidence.

MEN'S SWIMMING

1959-1970 *Wading in the Water*

In 1959 Phil Van Heest and a few other students who were swimming enthusiasts approached athletic director Barney Steen and asked that Calvin sponsor a swim team. In response to their request, a swim club was organized that same year.

The hardy souls making up that first club had no facilities readily available. Such practice as they were able to manage was held early in the morning in the tiny pool in the downtown YMCA. In 1960 Professor Carl Sinke was designated as the club's faculty mentor; Van Heest functioned as team leader. In 1961 Dick Katte, a recent graduate assisting in the Physical Education Department, was appointed as coach.

Dean of students Philip Lucasse followed Katte in 1961 and led the squad for the next four years. Lucasse wryly remembers meeting his swimmers at 6:00 a.m. for practice in the "Y's" 60-foot pool. Opponents back then included schools such as Grand Rapids Junior College, Schoolcraft Community College, Jackson Junior College, and Albion. After four years, Lucasse managed to convince Steen that

this program, with its group of loyal swimmers, should be elevated to varsity status.

Steen himself took over coaching responsibilities in 1966. Mark VerWys was his first ace swimmer, establishing an early record in the 50-yard freestyle in 1968. Two track and field stars were also members of the squad in the late 1960s: Rudy Vlaardingerbroek and Dave Ver Merris. Steen was still coach when swimming became a MIAA championship sport in 1971—three years before the new Calvin natatorium opened.

1971-1979 *Positive Strokes*

The first four years of Calvin's participation in MIAA swimming continued to be encumbered by the lack of facilities. During these years the team used the pool at East Grand Rapids High School for home meets and for practice, but because the high school's needs took priority, Calvin's men were forced to practice at ten o'clock in the evening. Nevertheless, the squad showed intermittent improvement during these years, winning no meets in the 1970-71 season, two in 1971-72, one again in 1972-73, but three in 1973-74, two of which were in MIAA competition.

BY THE SKIN OF HIS TOES

Late in the 1960s cross country runner Ron Nydam decided that running barefoot would improve his performance. He claims it actually did. But he hadn't reckoned with late fall Michigan weather when he resolved to discard his shoes.

One afternoon in November, after four inches of snow had fallen the night before, Calvin had an away meet with Hope. Undeterred by the snow, Nydam once again ran barefoot. He disregarded the numbness that gradually developed in his toes, only to discover a few days later that he had suffered frostbite in the race, and that skin was peeling from his big toe.

Unfortunately, Ron was also Coach Barney Steen's top diver on the swimming team, and Ron needed those big toes for sensitivity and balance. Only after six weeks of healing could he once again dive—and get out of Steen's doghouse.

The team continued to be small in number; at the close of the 1971 schedule only seven members received varsity letters. Four swimmers stood out during these first four years in the league. Diver Craig Van Der Veer placed second in the MIAA meet in 1971, while Dave Follett received all-league honors in 1972, Rick Feenstra in 1973, and Rick Steenwyk in 1974. Meanwhile, the Knights eagerly anticipated the completion of the Calvin pool.

The 1974-75 season was marked both by a new coach, as Jim Timmer, Sr. succeeded Barney Steen, and by the opening of the splendid new Bergsma Memorial Natatorium. The team responded appropriately, taking third place in the MIAA, its highest finish yet, and winning half of its meets

overall. For the first time Calvin placed two swimmers on the all-league squad: Ken Mange and Rick Steenwyk.

The next three seasons met with still greater success, as the squad placed second in the MIAA all three years. A number of exceptional swimmers distinguished themselves by earning all-league honors: Rick Feenstra for a second time, as well as Dave Cooke, Ken Koldenhoven, Dave Otten, Jim Mange, Tom Tabor, and Robert Reehoorn. Reehoorn was a double victor in the league championship meet in 1978, winning both the 500- and 1,650-yard freestyle events. During his remarkable career he established four Calvin records as well as the MIAA record in the 500-yard freestyle.

Although Reehoorn continued to stand out the following year, once again winning All-MIAA honors, Calvin's total performance sagged somewhat, as the team closed out the decade with a 3-6 record overall, while going 2-3 in the league.

1980-1989 High and Low Tides

The next four years saw three coaching changes. Mike Landis led the squad in 1979-80, Ron Chlasta was coach for the next two years, and Nancy Meyer was appointed to take over the program for the 1982-83 season. Though Reehoorn once again excelled and Dirk Pruis placed 11th nationally in one-meter diving, Landis' squad finished fifth in the league standings. Chlasta's teams finished third in 1980-81 and second the following year. Both years, Dirk Pruis placed seventh in one-meter diving at the NCAA nationals and received All-MIAA honors.

For the 1982-83 season Calvin's 15-man squad was coached by Nancy Meyer, who still today remains grateful for the assistance of Chuck Wilson and Scott Visser. She also recalls the splendid team leadership of captains Mark Swets and

Dirk Pruis

Tom Vanden Berg. Meyer's team did exceptionally well and finished second in the MIAA, due in part to freshman Steve Ruiter's remarkable achievements. Ruiter set no fewer than seven school records that year, and his teammates set another five. Little wonder that Ruiter, one of the premier swimmers in the history of the program, was named league MVP and became Calvin's first All-American in swimming.

Ken Mange assumed coaching responsibilities for the next seven years. His first two squads were very successful, losing a miserly total of two dual meets, as Ruiter continued his standout performances both in the league and in the NCAA championships. Charlie Vander Ploeg won All-MIAA team membership, and Bill Van Ee and Jeff Tanis led Calvin's divers.

The Knights maintained a winning record in the following season, 1985-86, but failed to do so the last three years of the decade. During those years only Vander Ploeg and Eric Danhof received all-league honors, Vander Ploeg for the fourth time. The decade ended with a bit of a drought.

1990-2003 Plunging Ahead

Calvin's swimmers enjoyed a measure of resurgence in the 1989-90 season, closing in third place, as Jeff Homan and Tom Marks led the team's efforts and won All-MIAA status, the latter distinction also being enjoyed by Alex Porte the following year.

During its first season under new coach Dan Baas, 1991-92, Calvin placed fourth in the league, as it had done the previous year. It repeated that finish the next two seasons as

well. The standout Calvin swimmer during that three-year period was Mike Lubbers, who eventually received All-MIAA and All-American honors three times. The 1994-95 and 1995-96 seasons were noteworthy only by virtue of the performances of Lubbers, Mike Shoemaker, and Mike Vander Laan, with Lubbers placing in three events in the 1996 national meet.

Dan Gelderloos was named Baas' successor for the 1996-97 season, a position he continues to hold. During most of his tenure, Calvin has placed in the middle in the MIAA standings. From 1997 to 2003 the Knights were a very respectable third in the league. Mike Vander Baan, Keith Ritsema, and Brad Flikkema led the squad from 1996 through 1999, with Vander Baan winning all-league honors four times, while Ritsema and Flikkema made the All-MIAA squad twice. A. J. Penninga was the only team member to be granted that honor for the 1999-2000 season.

Although unable to move upward in the MIAA, Calvin's swimmers did well in the NCAA standings the first three years after the beginning of the new millennium, finishing 18th in 2000-2001, 9th the following year, and 12th in 2002-2003. Although that success would not have been possible without the efforts of a number of solid performers, exceptional swimmers during those years were Peter Boumgarden, A. J. Penninga, Brad White, and Ryan Johnson, all of whom also were named to the all-league team. Calvin's strength those years was concentrated in the butterfly and freestyle events. With Coach Gelderloos' guidance, the squad looks forward to Boumgarden's continuing leadership in the coming season.

WOMEN'S SWIMMING

1979-1989 On Your Mark . . .

The 1978-79 season, the first for the women's swimming program under MIAA auspices, was not particularly auspicious. Both the team and their new coach, Nancy Meyer, were inexperienced. Thus it was no surprise when the squad tied Adrian for fifth place in the league with a 2-9 record. Symptomatic of the program's uncertain start was its 9:28.59 performance in the 800-yard relay, a time nearly two full minutes slower than today's record.

However, the next season already showed a measure of improvement. The team's dual meet record for the year was 4-6, and this time the Knights claimed fifth place alone. First-year students Vicky DeGroot, Deb Ruiter, and Cheryl Weaver showed real promise, as the squad set 19 new school records.

Progress continued the following year, as was evidenced by a 5-4 winning season, the first in the program's history, and a fourth-place league finish. Although the team had only seven swimmers and one diver, two of its members, freshman sprinter Cheri Feenstra and senior diver Susan Murphy, qualified for the NCAA championships.

The Knights repeated their fourth-place MIAA finish in 1982-83, tying Albion for second in the dual meets and narrowly losing to the Britons in the championships. Mary Otter, Deb Ruiter, Cathy Vila, and Cheryl Weaver made the all-league team, while Weaver, Feenstra, Vila, and Otter qualified for the NCAA meet.

Ken Mange succeeded Meyer as women's coach the following year, a position he retained through the 1985-86 season. All three of his teams had winning records, finishing 8-2 the first year, 9-1 the second, and 6-3 the third. The list of All-MIAA swimmers those years includes Mary Otter, Deb Ruiter, Cheryl Weaver, Sari Brummel, Karen Dekker, Liesl Vande Creek, Cathy Vila, and Anita Haynal. Mange's 1984-85 squad finished 17th at the NCAA meet; the following year, the team took 27th place. All-American honors during those years were won by diver Sari Brummel, Liesl Vande Creek in the 50-yard freestyle, and Karen Dekker in the 100-yard breaststroke.

Nancy Meyer returned as head coach of the team in 1986-87. Her second stint in the role was very different

Sari Brummel

from her first, for the Knight swimmers had improved in a number of areas. Benefiting greatly from the leadership of Mary Otter and Anita Haynal, the team finished second in the league. Sari Brummel dominated diving in the MIAA and also won All-American distinction, as did Stephanie Rhind in the breaststroke and Liesl Vande Creek Pruis in the sprints.

The following season showed only minor slippage, as the squad finished third in the league. However, it was blessed with several outstanding individual performers. Stephanie Rhind defended her league titles in the 100 and 200 breaststroke and became a repeat All-American, as did Liesl Pruis. Joining them in receiving All-American honors were Sally Vannette and Laura Lantinga.

The 1988-89 season, the last in the decade, produced yet another third-place finish in the MIAA for Meyer's team, as it posted a 7-5 dual-meet record overall. The team set four new school records and, at season's end, included three all-league, All-American members: Stephanie Rhind once again in the breaststroke, Patti Van Andel in the sprints, and the versatile Jacki Belyea. The decade had begun with struggle, but it ended with a program that had proved its mettle.

1990-2003 Improving Lap by Lap

The 1989-90 season was Meyer's last as head swimming coach. Once again the team did well, earning yet another third-place finish in the MIAA. As had been the case the prior year, the squad set four new school records, and Van Andel, Rhind, Belyea, and Miriam Vos won All-American status in the 200-yard medley relay.

The following year Ken Mange, who had coached the team from 1983 until 1986 and had served as Meyer's assistant, returned to the program. The 1990-91 squad was unable to match the achievements of its immediate predecessors, winning two dual meets while losing four and finding itself in fourth place in the MIAA at the end of the season. Jackie Belyea continued to stand out, however, making the All-MIAA team for the third consecutive year.

Mary Schutten became the program's next coach, assum-

ing her duties with the 1991-92 season. The four years of her tenure saw a fifth-place league finish the first two seasons, third-place standing the next, and fourth place in 1993-94 and 1994-95. Her teams were noted for their balance and for two stellar individual performers. In 1992-93 Jennifer Cole was named to the All-MIAA team, and in 1993-94 freshman Kathleen Shaughnessy won All-American recognition in the 200 butterfly and earned honorable mention status in the 100 butterfly as well.

Calvin, under new coach Deanna Fridley, was firmly lodged in fourth place for still another year, as the 1995-96 swimmers repeated their performance of the two previous seasons. However, the Knights did set three school records at the conference championships. In addition, Kristi Van Woerkom, an outstanding swimmer, took the MIAA title in the 100-yard freestyle with a time of 54.70 and was named to the all-league team.

Better days were close at hand, however, as Dan Gelderloos, a former four-year member of the Calvin men's swimming team, took over coaching responsibilities for the 1996-97 season.

Improvement was not immediate, as his first team slipped to fifth place in the MIAA. However, Kristi Van Woerkom continued her superb swimming, winning the league title in the 100-yard freestyle with a time of 53.81. Both Van Woerkom and Leslie Harris received all-league recognition. The 1997-98 squad did just a bit better at the MIAA level, finishing fourth, with Van Woerkom once again winning All-MIAA honors, swimming the 500-yard freestyle in a fine time of 5:15.94.

The 1998-99 team was another story, as it finished a solid second place in both the dual and league meets and registered a number of striking individual performances. MIAA champions included Van Woerkom in the 500- and 200-yard freestyle events, Kara Davidson in three-meter diving, Liesje Konyndyk in the 1,650 freestyle, and Erin Kloostra, Kaity Conrad, Erica Smith, and Van Woerkom in the 400-yard freestyle medley. Gaining places on the All-MIAA team were Kloostra, Van Woerkom, Davidson, Konyndyk, and Smith. Special recognition should be given Kristi Van Woerkom, a superlative athlete who gained All-American status in both track and field and in swimming in the same year—a truly notable feat.

Despite the loss of Van Woerkem due to graduation, the team continued its excellent league performance in the 1999-2000 season, repeating its second-place finish of the year before. Once again, the team's effort featured league championships in both individual and relay events. Anne Kuiper led the MIAA in the 200-yard individual medley, while Calvin again won league titles in two relay events, as Conrad, Kloostra, Kuiper, and Katie Nagelkirk were victorious in both the 200-yard and 400-yard freestyle relays. All-league recognition was given Ginni Baker, Nagelkirk, Conrad, Kloostra, Kuiper, and Konyndyk.

The league championship that had eluded the Knights for some 12 years finally became theirs during the stellar 2000-2001 season, as Calvin finished first in the MIAA championships and second in the dual-meet season. The two victorious relay teams of the season before won a second league title; in addition, Brittney Stevens joined Nagelkirk, Kuiper, and Kloostra as they took the 200-yard medley re-lay. Individual MIAA champions included Nagelkirk in the 50- and 100-yard freestyle and Ginni Baker in the 400-yard individual medley. All-league honors were won by Baker, Kloostra, Konyndyk, Kuiper, Nagelkirk, and Mara McGuin, and the team finished a creditable 18th in the Division III championships.

The 2001-2002 season was the first in which the MIAA championship was determined by the results of the league meet only. Although Calvin came in second to Hope in that contest, the Knights won a second consecutive title when the Dutch had to forfeit their championship due to the use of an ineligible swimmer. A host of Calvin swimmers did well. The 200-yard freestyle relay unit set a MIAA record of 1:36.82, the 400-yard freestyle relay swimmers won their event, and the 200- and 400-yard medley relay teams also came in first. Mara McGuin took the 400-yard individual medley, and Katie Nagelkirk dominated in the 50-yard freestyle, setting a league record in the process; Nagelkirk also won the title in the 100- and 200-yard freestyle events. At the close of another very successful season, Kloostra, McGuin, Nagelkirk, Conrad, and Brittney Stevens were chosen for the All-MIAA team, with Nagelkirk selected as the league's Most Valuable Swimmer.

After two years of conference championships, Calvin finished as runner-up in the MIAA in 2002-2003. This time both the individual performers and the relay teams stood out. The Knights won both the 200- and 400-yard freestyle relays. Individual champions included Sara Ter Haar, the three-meter diving champion; Abby Johnson, who took the 200-yard butterfly and set a league record of 4:37.25 in the 400-yard individual medley; and the redoubtable Katie Nagelkirk, who in addition to participating in both winning relay teams, won the 50-, 100-, and 200-yard freestyle, setting an MIAA record in both of the latter two events. It was no surprise that Nagelkirk, concluding her magnificent career at Calvin, was named the league's Most Valuable Swimmer for the second consecutive year.

After a modest beginning a quarter-century earlier, the women's swimming program clearly has established itself as a consistent force in the conference.

WOMEN'S TENNIS

1953-1960 A New Racket

With its entry into the WMIAA, Calvin began to concentrate on developing a competitive women's tennis team. Records for the first seven years are incomplete, but we do know that early on, Coach Nell Oosthoek's squad scheduled dual matches with Aquinas, Hope, and Kalamazoo, defeating Hope twice in the spring of 1956. That same year, the team traveled to Kalamazoo College for the annual WMIAA Field Day, upsetting favored Kalamazoo and tying the Hornets for the co-championship. Two of the team leaders that year were Marge Vandenbosch and Trudy Bonnema, who won the league doubles title.

Bev Klooster

Three years later, the Knights, now coached by Ellen Rottman, repeated their gritty performance of 1956, surprising Kalamazoo College by winning another co-championship at the Field Day. This time it was Phyllis Zandee and Bev Klooster who won the doubles competition. Both of the co-championships won in the 1950s represented significant achievements in this early phase of women's tennis at Calvin.

1960-1969 Aces and Outs

Calvin may not have won the league title in the early years of the new decade, but two players did win the WMIAA's Sue Little Memorial Award for sportsmanship. Ardie DeVries was given this honor in 1962; the following year it was earned by Karen Timmer.

1964 witnessed improvement in the squad's performance. Led by Coach Winifred Byker, the Knights took the league title, winning both the singles and doubles championship at the WMIAA tournament in Adrian. Team leaders that year were Diane DeBoer, Mary Groot, and Karen Timmer. The 1965 season was also successful, as Calvin, now coached by Doris Zuidema, posted a 5-1 record, but the following two years saw less satisfying, identical 3-4 results, as newly appointed coach

Karen Timmer's team struggled. Annelies Knoppers became Timmer's successor in 1968; records indicate that in the final year of the decade the squad took fourth place in the conference, winning three matches while losing six.

1970-1979 Holding Serve

Calvin did well the first three years of the 1970s, and less well in 1973. In 1970 the Knights completed their dual meet schedule with a 6-2 record and tied Alma for second place in the final WMIAA standings, as Karen Langeland and Donna Afman won their flights in the league tournament. 1971 saw Calvin win seven matches and lose none, while the 1972 squad won four matches and lost an identical number—one of those losses being to Michigan State University. Coach Knoppers' team finished third in that season's tournament. 1973, however, witnessed a bit of slippage, as Calvin could do no better than a 5-5 record and fourth place in conference standings. The final year of Knoppers' coaching tenure, 1974, saw the Lady Knights move up one notch, to third place, as Jane Huizenga won the Sue Little Award.

For the 1975 and 1976 seasons Karla Hoesch Wolters led the women's tennis program. Her 1975 the team finished a solid third in the WMIAA tournament. Despite posting a 6-1 record in dual-match play, Calvin placed fourth in the league tournament in 1976.

Nancy Van Noord succeeded Hoesch in 1977 and directed the women's program for the next three years. An overall 6-2 record and a first-place finish at the WMIAA championships marked Van Noord's first year of coaching. The following season, Calvin finished its schedule with a fine 8-1 record overall and second place in the league standings. Among the team's stalwarts that year were Debbie Broene and Patti Doezema, MIAA champions in the first doubles flight, and Mary Whiting, who played in the first singles slot. The squad also won second place in the state tournament and finished third in the regionals. In the last year of Van Noord's tenure as coach, the team's overall win-loss record was 6-3, with Calvin winning the SMAIAW championship and Joan Hosner winning her flight in MIAA play.

1980-1989 Aces in Places

As the decade began, Nancy Meyer took Van Noord's place as head coach of Calvin's team, holding that position for three years, just as her two predecessors had. Meyer, who had only a casual interest in tennis prior to her appointment, continues to acknowledge with gratitude the help she got from her assistant, Denise Zoeterman, that first year.

The squad had notable success during the three years of Meyer's coaching tenure. In 1980, the first year that the team took a spring break trip to the South, Calvin was runner-up to Hope College and qualified for regionals. The Knights repeated their second place finish in 1981, but achieved a co-championship with Hope in 1982, the final season in which Meyer served as coach. Among Calvin's stalwart players during those years were Mary Whiting and Cheryl Van Baren.

In 1983 Nancy Van Noord returned as women's tennis coach, remaining in that capacity until 1987. The team registered solid performances in the first two years of her coaching, becoming the conference runner-up in 1983 and taking third place in 1984. During those successful years Jan Boerema, Carol Voren-

Tawnie Knottnerus

kamp, and Tawnie Knottnerus distinguished themselves by their excellent play, and Jan Boerema received the Sue Little Award in both 1983 and 1984. In 1985 Knottnerus won the distinction of being named Calvin's only MVP in tennis in five decades, as the squad managed a 3-3 league record. However, the following year proved to be a long one. Hit hard by the graduation of some of its best players, the 1986 team posted a 1-4 record. The struggle continued in 1987, as Calvin took fourth place in the MIAA.

For the next seven years Dean Ellens coached the team.

From 1988 to 1990 the squad was unable to finish higher than fourth in the league. Indicative of Calvin's challenges was the fact that only one player, Joni Faber, advanced to the tournament finals during that three-year span.

1990-2003 *Volleys and Victories*

Although the team was unable to move up in the MIAA standings in 1991, Julie Kuzee became Calvin's first individual champion since 1985. In 1992 Ellens' squad finally snapped its record of having finished fourth for seven consecutive years. By virtue of a strong performance in the tournament, the Knights managed a third-place league finish, an achievement they repeated the next year as well. Team leaders those two years were Betty Williams and Debbie Pettinga. 1994's relatively young team dropped back one notch, to fourth place in the league standings.

Marie Van Tubbergen coached Calvin the following year. Under her leadership the squad won half of its games, neither gaining nor losing ground to MIAA opponents. Dean Ellens resumed coaching the Knights for the 1996 and 1997 seasons. The first year after his return, the squad had a fine 15-5 overall record, but could do no better than two wins and three losses in league play. Though not outstanding, 1997 was another generally satisfying year, as the team compiled a 12-8 overall record and tied with Albion for third place in the league. Leading the team in those two years were a number of players: Bekah Biel, Mandy Sytsma, Kathleen Konyndyk, Allison De Wys, Anita Van Eerden, and Tracy Shook.

In 1998 Kim Gall succeeded Ellens as coach. Although the season saw a 15-4 overall win-loss record and a league record of 6-2, a fourth-place performance in the tournament resulted in fourth place in the final standings. Senior Allison DeWys received a dual honor, as she was both named to the All-MIAA first team and selected for the Sue Little Award. Other strong contributors that year were Mandy Sytsma and Heidi Thatcher.

Calvin moved up one notch in the league standings in 1999, due to a strong performance in the tournament. Among the highlights of that successful season was the Intercollegiate Tennis Association's naming of Bekah Biel as scholar-athlete, an honor awarded to no other MIAA tennis player in 1999. Mandy Sytsma and Tracy Shook also played key roles in the team's success.

The year 2000 saw another excellent performance by the team. Attaining a 16-4 record overall and going 6-1 in league dual-match play, the Knights tied with St. Mary's for second place in the MIAA. Among the season's highlights was Calvin's participation in the Midwest Invitational Tournament in Madison, Wisconsin. Although the competition was stiff, it afforded team members valuable experience. A number of players, including Katie Zeilstra and Kait Disselkoen, contributed to the season's fine success.

With the onset of the 2001 season, the tennis program saw yet another coaching change, as Jerry Bergsma succeeded Kim Gall. The Knights performed very respectably under their new coach, compiling an 11-5 overall record and going 4-3 in conference matches. These statistics are just a bit misleading, however, since Calvin lost three matches by a 4-5 score. In large measure because of these losses, Calvin finished fourth in the final MIAA standings. Both Kait Disselkoen and Sally Skodinski enjoyed an exceptional year of competition in 2001.

Skodinski continued her fine play the following year, as Calvin once again earned a tie for fourth in the conference. Counterbalancing a somewhat disappointing dual-match outcome was an outstanding performance in the tournament at year's end. The 2003 season saw the team slip one notch downward in final MIAA standings, as it completed the season in fifth place. Notable for that year was the play of Sally Skodinski and Amy Zeilstra.

MEN'S TENNIS

1954-1959 Six Years, Four Coaches

With the exception of a brief interruption occasioned by the war years, Calvin had had a men's tennis team since 1931. However, MIAA membership introduced a new phase of the program.

The 1954 season was characterized by both continuity and change. The continued coaching of Albert Muyskens, affectionately known by the Calvin community as "Coochie," provided continuity; entry into the MIAA provided change. Roger Boerema played the number one position, while newcomers filled most of the additional slots. That first year of league membership saw Calvin finish in fourth place—a solid achievement.

Under their new coach, Gordon Buter, the Knights duplicated their fourth-place finish in 1955. Boerema continued to anchor the team, whose additional players included Dave Schreur, Jim Kok, Rich Sharda, and Roger Boer. Symptomatic of Kalamazoo's dominance in the sport, which continues to this day, was the fact that Sharda's defeat of Kalamazoo's number four singles player was celebrated as a singular achievement.

The 1956 and 1957 teams were coached by Albert Lewen, Calvin's director of food services. The team's first year under Lewen saw a fourth-place finish in the league, while the Knights slipped to fifth in 1957. Bill Kooistra, Bill Doezema, and Ed Meyering contributed significantly to Calvin's effort. As had been the case for many years, home matches were played at Franklin Park, today known as Martin Luther King Park.

History professor Howard Rienstra became men's coach in 1958 and continued in that position through the spring of 1961. Joining the squad for the 1958 season were Ken Zandee, Warren Boer, Ron Vanden Berg, and John DeHoog. A 3-6 league record meant another fifth place finish. The 1959 team had three freshman players: Phil Dommisse, Dave Flietstra, and John Musch. Their inexperience was no doubt one factor in Calvin's sixth-place finish that year.

1960-1969 Serving Up Success

In terms of wins and losses, the beginning of the new decade saw pronounced improvement in the program. Buttressing Calvin's effort were newcomers Ken Oosterhouse, Dave Vander

COOCHIE DISAPPEARS

Coochie Muyskens, Calvin's venerable, affable tennis coach in the early 1950s, seemed very relaxed, but appearances were deceiving. A particularly tense contest with Hope showed just how deceptive those appearances could be.

The final doubles match that afternoon would determine the winner and loser for the day. Featuring the best players on both teams, Jim Doezema and Al Peelen for Calvin, and Ron Bos and Warren Exoo for Hope, the game was played with abandon. Tension mounted as first one team prevailed, then the other.

Soon after the completion of the first set, team members became very concerned. Coochie had disappeared. After a careful search, Jim Kok found him seated behind the wheel of his 1947 Chevrolet, smoking cigarettes. Upon questioning, Coochie admitted that he had gotten too nervous to watch the match. Calvin eventually won, but without Coochie in the stands. A close match as such could perhaps be endured, but a close match against Hope?

Roger Boer

trip, a second new feature of the season was Calvin's hosting home matches on the newly completed Knollcrest courts.

The following year, 1963, saw a repeat of the previous season, as Calvin once again finished behind Hope and Kalamazoo in the MIAA. Ken Oosterhouse continued his fine play, while Dave Vander Hart won the first flight singles championship and was granted the league's Allen B. Stowe Award for sportsmanship.

Dave Vander Hart

The loss of Vander Hart and Oosterhouse due to graduation meant that the 1964 squad had to rely heavily on freshmen. However, newcomers Jim Edson, Bert DeLeeuw, Peter DeJong, Joel DeKoning, and Tom Prince came through, joining veterans Dick Bultman and Gord Vanderbrug and enabling the Knights to once again finish in third place in the MIAA.

Zuidema's 1965 squad dropped a notch in final league standings, as Albion replaced the Knights in third place. Despite the team's fourth-place MIAA finish, Dick Bultman was selected to receive the Stowe Award, becoming the second Calvin player to be granted this signal honor. The following year, the Knights, led by DeLeeuw, DeKoning, Prince, Don Klop, and Phil and John Stielstra, regained third place. This time it was Bert DeLeeuw who was given the Stowe Award. The fact that four Calvin players won this award in the 1960s

Hart, and Gord Vander Brug, who joined veterans Flietstra, Musch, and Dommisse. The 1960 team compiled a 7-2 league record, while the 1961 squad moved to second place in the MIAA, winning nine matches and losing only to Kalamazoo.

Calvin continued its excellent play in 1962, this time under the direction of Coach Marv Zuidema, who was almost inadvertently thrust into this role. Benefiting for the first time from a spring trip, the team finished with a 10-2 overall record and secured third place in the conference, behind co-champions Hope and Kalamazoo. In addition to the spring attests to the exceptional sportsmanship showed by several of Calvin's leading players.

1967 marked another change in the program, as Don Vroon began his 30-year tenure as coach of men's tennis. His first squad, composed of DeLeeuw, Ben Pekelder, Jim Bolt, Don Klop, Dave Post, and John DeVries, repeated the third-place performance of the previous year. The following two seasons, as the decade came to a close, Calvin was able to retain that standing in the league. Among newcomers contributing to the team's continuing success were John Lappenga, Jim Bolt, and Mark Van Faasen.

1970-1979 *Strong Sets*

As the decade of the 1970s began, Vroon firmly established himself as tennis coach by virtue of his dedication to the sport and his enthusiastic coaching. Not only did he lead Calvin's program, but he also was active in tennis circles in the MIAA, the greater Grand Rapids area, and the National Under 18 Tournament held annually in Kalamazoo.

Calvin's teams of the 1970s were always competitive, winning at least half of their matches and placing either second, third, or fourth in the conference, as Kalamazoo added to its unbroken string of MIAA championships. Typically, it was Calvin, Hope, Albion, or Alma battling for the runner-up position.

Among standouts during the early 1970s were Pekelder, Van Faasen, Greg Broene, Dick Frens, Bill Hop, Scott Feringa, and Al Van Den Bosch. In the middle of the decade Dave Knibbe, Steve House, Howard Hoff, and Dean Ellens led the team. Prominent players in the late 1970s were, among others, Dave Hartman, Tom Yonker, and Neil Jasperse. All-MIAA honors during that 10-year span were awarded to Pekelder, Van Faasen, Ellens, and

Dave Hartman

Hartman, while Greg Broene was named both an all-league player and the recipient of the prestigious Stowe Award.

1980-1989 *Chasing Hornets*

The 1980s were, in a sense, marked by "more of the same," as Calvin never sank lower than fifth place and usually ranked somewhat higher. Although Vroon continued to tell his players that Kalamazoo could be beaten, his team never supplanted the Hornets as league champion. The Knights generally won more games than they lost and usually challenged for the city championship.

A listing of talented team members who generally played in the top flights during these years includes, among others, Dave and Dan Hartman, Dave Kingma, Jim Doezema, Jeff Van De Vusse, Bill Stout, Jim Peterson, Joe Hollemans, Tom Wolff, Tom Zandee, Mark Knottnerus, Mark Lenters, and Alex Vander Pol. Dave Hartman stood out individually, winning All-MIAA honors for four consecutive years. It was Vroon's conviction that, on the collegiate level, the caliber of tennis play continued to steadily improve during the 1980s.

1990-2003 *Still Chasing*

Calvin's teams performed a remarkable feat by taking second place in the conference each year from 1990 through 1998. Given Kalamazoo's continuing dominance, achieving a second-place finish seemed at times to be nearly tantamount to winning the league title. Among the highlights of those years was Steve DeWeerd's second flight MIAA championship in 1995.

The teams' overall strength was mirrored in the number of individual players honored by the league. Winning first team All-MIAA honors were Mark Lenters in 1990, Alex Vander Pol in 1991, Brad Sytsma in 1992 and 1993, and John Knoester from 1992 to 1995. Steve DeWeerd received that honor twice, in 1995 and 1996, and Dave Meester won it in 1998. In addition, both DeWeerd and Knoester participated in the NCAA Division III tournament in 1993. Vroon's final years as coach obviously were highly productive.

John Knoester

A number of Calvin players also won MIAA awards on the basis of their sportsmanship or academic performance. Knoester received the Stowe Award in 1995, and Meester won it in 1998. Recipients of the "Doc" Green Award for academic excellence were Jeff Admiraal in 1994, Dan Meester in 1995, and Jon Vander Ark in 1997.

Don Vroon continued to coach the tennis team through the 1997 season, staying on for an additional year after his retirement from the faculty. For thirty years he gave Calvin's program stability, enthusiastic leadership, and dedicated service. His notable contributions were reflected not only in terms of matches won or lost, but also in the spirit with which he did his work.

Dean Ellens, college registrar, coached the squad for the next two seasons. Once again, Calvin's teams were competitive and performed well in the MIAA, finishing second in 1998 and fourth in 1999. Dave Meester distinguished himself in 1998 by being named to the all-league team and winning the Stowe Award.

From the 2000 season through 2003, Milan Norgauer filled in as tennis coach while he worked on his doctoral degree. Calvin continued its solid play under his leadership, three times completing its schedule in third place in the MIAA. Several fine young players entered the program in 2002 and 2003, among them Kevin Van Haitsma, who played first singles and was selected for the all-conference team for three consecutive years.

At the conclusion of the 2003 season John Ross, a member of the Physical Education Department staff, was appointed tennis coach. Coach Ross, whose last experience was at Earlham College, is a seasoned and knowledgeable teacher of the game. With a new coach and an infusion of several gifted young players, Calvin's program appears to be set for the immediate future.

MEN'S TRACK AND FIELD

Editor's note: Especially the latter half of this historical summary highlights to a great extent the achievements of outstanding athletes and All-Americans. Given space restrictions and the total number of team members who participated in the program, such an emphasis is difficult to avoid. However, any successful track and field effort also relies on the dedicated runners and field event men who win second-, third-, fourth-, or fifth-place points and help keep the team concept alive. All such contributors also have our deep respect and appreciation.

1953-1959 *In the Starting Blocks*

Upon entering the MIAA in 1953, Calvin had meager experience in track and field and had to work against significant disadvantages. To begin with, the Knights had no facilities of their own and had to rely on practice areas rented from the Grand Rapids Public Schools. Holding practice sessions was a challenge, since Calvin had to work around the schedule of local schools—in particular, Ottawa Hills High School, located a half-mile south of the Franklin campus. The Knights could use the Ottawa track only before 3:00 p.m., and home meets at Houseman or South Field had to be held either before or after high school practice sessions. Since those times were inconvenient, it was difficult to find officials to run the meets.

Furthermore, the facilities and equipment, when compared to today's layouts, were distinctly primitive. Running tracks had cinder surfaces and were not always carefully maintained. Shot put and discus surfaces also were composed of cinders, and high jump and pole vault pits were filled with a mixture of sawdust and sand. The shaft of wooden javelins that were not properly thrown would crack on contact with

the ground, and hurdlers who hit the heavy Gill hurdles and fell would find cinders painfully embedded in their shins, knees, torsos, and arms.

Neither Barney Steen nor Dave Tuuk of Calvin's Physical Education Department could do anything about the inadequate, cramped locker rooms in the old dormitory, but they did improvise as best they could in regard to practice facilities, creating some field event pits on the East Campus located on Ethel and Franklin streets. At least weight men and jumpers could now work out without scheduling restrictions.

Calvin's first season in the MIAA was not particularly auspicious; the Knights had few performers who could compete successfully against athletes from Albion and Hope, in particular. Dual meets with Adrian, Olivet, Alma, and Kalamazoo were not catastrophic for Calvin during those early years, but Hope had an established, successful program, and Albion once defeated Calvin by the score of 122-9. Despite the difficult early going, Tuuk remained confident that, given time and improved facilities, the Knights would soon be able to measure up.

Dual meets did not count toward the final standings, which were determined solely on the basis of performances at the MIAA Field Day at Kalamazoo College's Angell Field. Driving to Kalamazoo by car, the only means of transportation available, was an adventure in itself in those pre-freeway days, as the caravan wended its way through Moline, Wayland, Bradley, Plainwell, Cooper, and the like.

The Field Day itself was quite an event. One of its features was an elected queen who represented each competing institution and presented medals to the event winners as they stood on the awards stand. Some of the events themselves bordered on the farcical—in particular, the 440-yard dash, which was curiously staged and saw a good deal of pushing and shoving, becoming in essence an exercise in the survival of the fittest.

During those early years, Calvin did have a few veterans who could score in the big meet. Elton "Tiny" Koops was competitive in the weights, Morrie Tubergen in the 880 and mile run, Pete Duyst in the 440 and relay, and Stan Koster in the high jump, pole vault, and javelin. Duane Vander Brug from Detroit ran the sprints and both hurdle events, Al Vander Griend threw the discus, and Wayne Gritter was a high jumper. Sprinter Rich Hertel, javelin thrower Mel Veenema, and accomplished hurdler Gerry Holwerda joined the team a year or two later and were able to win points at the Field Day. Despite the efforts of these athletes, however, over the first few years, the Knights were fortunate to score 15 or 20 points in the course of the entire meet, which placed them in the middle of the final league standings.

Not until the late 1950s, as the cross country program gradually developed, did better-conditioned runners and field men begin fill the team's ranks, among them Koster in the javelin, shot-putter Dave Altena, weight man Ralph Honderd, and pole vaulter and hurdler Ken Tanis. As time went on, Calvin was able to field athletes who could challenge for first place in nearly every event, and the team also had the depth necessary to pick up additional fourth- or fifth-place points. Tuuk was gaining confidence that Knight talent and desire were winning out over Spartan facilities. That confidence seemed warranted, as in the spring of 1959 Calvin came within one point of defeating both Hope and Kalamazoo in dual meets.

1960-1969 Sprinting into Contention

After mixed success in the 1960 dual-meet season, the Knights once again journeyed to Kalamazoo for the MIAA conference meet. Tuuk's squad was fairly balanced, having strength in a number of areas. Solid performers included Altena and Honderd in the weights, Koster in the javelin, and Vander Griend in the high jump. Ken Tanis ran both hurdles, Wayne DeYoung ran the 440, and cross country runners Jim De Bie, Barry Koops, Al Bierling, and Dan Achtyes were strong in the distance events. However, the Knights were weak in the sprints, where Mike Oostendorp was their only threat.

With every athlete giving his very best, the scrappy Calvin squad captured first place, defeating runner-up Kalamazoo by a scant two points. After a long climb throughout the 1950s, the Knights won their first MIAA championship in track and field, and without a home track! This first league title—the result of combined, determined, spirited effort—continues to stand out and shine brightly in the history of the sport at Calvin.

If anyone suspected that the Knights of 1960 were only a "flash in the pan," the next three years proved them wrong. Distance runners Koops and DeBie were back for their senior year in 1961 and finished strong, as Koops set MIAA records in both the mile (4:21.7) and two mile (9:49.2). Ralph Honderd, having recovered from a broken arm, established a new league record in the shot put at 48'5", Sandy Leestma placed in both the 100- and 220-yard dashes, and Walt Pruiksma and Mike DeYoung came in first and third in the 440. Vander Griend took the high jump title, and Calvin's mile relay team won the final running event of the day. This time, the Knights defeated runner-up Albion by a margin of 66 $\frac{2}{3}$–49 $\frac{2}{3}$.

Kalamazoo furnished the primary opposition in 1962, but Calvin once again overcame, defeating the Hornets in the decisive conference meet, 84 $\frac{1}{2}$–54 $\frac{1}{2}$. Ray Hommes replaced DeBie and Koops in the distance events and was a double victor in the mile and two mile. Leestma excelled in the 100, DeYoung in the 440, and Al Bierling in the 880. Calvin took four firsts in the field events, with Vander Griend (high jump), George Zuiderveen (pole vault), John Advocaat (discus), and Denny Duimstra (shot put) each claiming first place. As in the year previous, the Knights once again concluded the day with a victory in the mile relay. An additional 11 team members contributed with second-, third-, fourth-, and fifth-place finishes to help swell the point total.

The 1963 conference meet was held at the fine new Knollcrest facility, and Calvin did not disappoint its fans. Once again strong in the weight events, the Knights' Duimstra, Pete Winkle, and Jim Wynstra took the first three places in the shot put, while Advocaat, Winkle, and Duimstra all scored in the discus. Versatile George Zuiderveen won points in the pole vault, high jump, and 220-yard low hurdles; Jim Remeur placed in both hurdle events; and Walt Pruiksma came out on top in the 440. Leestma and Stan Klop did well in the sprints; Nelson Miedema, Al Zietsma, and Lou Mensonides took the first three spots in the two mile; and Hommes won both the 880 and mile run. The result was a 77½–51 victory over runner-up Albion.

Although Hommes and Wynstra continued their stellar performances in 1964 and Calvin showed substantial depth in a number of areas, the Knights fell one point short in the conference meet, losing 59-58 to Albion. Klop, Advocaat, Remeur, Paul Jansma, Lou Hekman, and Ben Snoeyink all did well, but weakness in the sprints hurt Calvin's cause. Despite that narrow defeat, the year had seen some very fine achievements and was an overall success.

Albion repeated its MIAA championship in 1965, while the Knights edged Hope to come in second. The team showed power in the weight events and distances, and Ben Snoeyink set a record in the intermediate hurdles, but with Dave Ver Merris' injury, the team was not able to compete successfully in the sprints.

The absence of outstanding distance runners and weight men crippled Calvin's cause in 1966, as the Knights slipped to fourth place. Bill DeHorn jumped 6'4", De Leeuw and Hekman

WHEN THE SMOKE(S) ALMOST CLEARED

It was a home track meet at Knollcrest in 1962, with Orville Vander Griend, Calvin's top high jumper, competing. Typically, Vander Griend would keep jumping in his sweat suit until the opposition was eliminated. At this meet he made a jump at approximately 6', when a pack of cigarettes fell out of his sweat top. Eventually, this little mishap got back to the coach, who levied no penalty, but said, "Orville, without the cigs you could go up to 6'6"." Case closed.

took two places in the javelin, and the mile relay team of Klop, Jay Eppinga, Sander de Haan, and Ver Merris tied the MIAA record. However, despite such bright spots, the team's overall performance fell short of that of previous years.

The Knights of 1967 showed definite improvement. A major reason for their stronger showing was the arrival of Rudy Vlaardingerbroek, one of the greatest weight men in Calvin track and field history. Complementing his performance was that of a healthy Dave Ver Merris, who ran a 48.4 in the 440 and anchored the mile relay team, which set a record with a time of 3:21.9. Joining Ver Merris in that run were Joel Vander Male, Denny Van Andel, and Sandy de Haan. Dave Heth, who had transferred from Albion, broke his own record of the year previous, vaulting 13'10". Despite such fine individual showings that year, Hope was the dominant force in the league.

For the 1968 season the MIAA format in track and field was changed, so that the results of both dual meets and the conference meet counted for the championship. Although Calvin, led by Vlaardingerbroek, won all six of its dual tests, Hope narrowly defeated the Knights in the conference, thus sharing the MIAA title with Tuuk's squad. Among the year's

Rudy Vlaardingerbroek

high points were Ver Merris' exemplary achievements in the 440 and the record-setting quarter-mile relay of Dave Vander Goot, Jim Van Orman, Larry Baar, and Denny Van Andel.

As in 1968, the Knights convincingly won all of their dual meets in 1969, but this time they also defeated all opponents in the conference meet held at Hope. Vlaardingerbroek concluded his superlative career as a Knight by setting new MIAA records in the shot, discus, and javelin, and he also took third place in the high hurdles—all in all, a truly exceptional achievement. Other high points of the day included victories in both relays and Jack Vander Male's success in the high jump, intermediate hurdles, and the mile relay. It was a great season for a Calvin team blessed with exceptional senior athletes and was a splendid way to end the decade of the 1960s, when Calvin emerged from the shadows to win a total of six league titles.

1970-1979 Slow Start, Strong Finish

The first Calvin track and field team of the 1970s suffered from the loss of several key athletes, chief among them being Rudy Vlaardingerbroek. As a result, the team only barely resembled the magnificent 1969 squad. Joel Vander Male was

the Knights' only first-place winner, hurdlers were virtually non-existent, and only a handful of second- and third-place performances helped keep Calvin's score respectable. Tuuk's squad tumbled to fourth place in the league standings, as Alma took the championship.

The situation improved significantly the following year, however. Randy Veltkamp, a talented middle-distance runner from Timothy Christian near Chicago, and his teammate, George Van Kampen, gave the team new impetus, as did a solid quartet of sprinters: John Rottschafer, Don Otten, Jim Eldersveld, and Larry Baar. Veltkamp ran excellent times, winning both the 880 and the mile; he also anchored the victorious mile relay team. The trio of Ron Flietstra and Ron and Bob Bosch also took the first three places in the discus. John DeJonge won the long jump competition, and Calvin's sprinters came in first in the 440 relay with a fine time of 42.2. Propelled by this infusion of new energy, the Knights lost only to Alma in the dual-meet season and placed a solid second in the conference meet.

In 1972 Gordon Brewer, Hope College's track coach, assembled a talented team that won the championship trophy. Calvin did well in its dual meet with Hope, losing by only seven points, and placed a solid second in final MIAA standings. John DeJonge once again was victor in the long jump, the Bosch brothers, Ron and Bob, did well in the shot put and discus, and Ev Van Der Heide aided the cause by scoring in the javelin, but the Knights' overall performance was hurt by the absence of the solid sprint group of the previous year.

During the spring break of 1973 the track and field team made its first training trip to the South. Although only half of the team members were able to go, the experience was invaluable for the development of camaraderie. Meets with Austin Peay of Clarksville, Tennessee and Pensacola Junior College were among the trip's highlights.

That same year, Calvin hosted the MIAA championships at Knollcrest. Fielding a strong team with considerable depth, the Knights completed their dual-meet season undefeated and scored an impressive 79 points to take the conference title as well. Ron Bosch, Gregg Afman, John

DeJonge, and Ron Vander Pol all took first place in their events; team captain George Van Kampen was stellar in the 880 and placed second in the mile run, in addition to anchoring the winning mile relay team. Appropriately enough, Van Kampen was elected league MVP.

Alma was to furnish Calvin's chief opposition in 1974, defeating the Knights in the dual meet between the two schools. As a result, Calvin entered the conference championships as the underdog. Only Afman and Veurink placed first, but surprising performances by a number of Knight athletes such as Ben Beversluis, Keith Bode, Mike Volkema, Phil Breems, Dick Vanden Berg, Stan Hiemenga, Joel Apol, Mike De Young, and Pete Vander Werff kept Calvin in contention until the decisive event of the day, the mile relay, which would determine the meet victor. After tenacious laps run by DeYoung, Hiemenga, and Van Kampen, Ben Beversluis, running the anchor leg, nosed out Alma's fourth runner to clinch the meet for Tuuk's squad. This 1974 conference meet was one of the most exciting in the entire history of the sport at Calvin.

The Knights repeated as champions in each of the next four years, from 1975 through 1978. Though the team showed considerable depth in various events, strength in the sprints—featuring Gary "Speedy" Mulder, Jim Eldersveld, Dwight Doezema, and Joel Cooper, and the gifted mile relay team of Doezema, Cooper, Timmer, and Beversluis—was particularly notable in the 1975 season, as was Afman's fifth-place in the NCAA Division III national meet.

The 1976 season duplicated that of 1975, as Calvin won all its dual meets and clearly outdistanced the rest of the league in the conference meet. Both the mile relay team, composed this time of Beversluis, Cooper, Jon Houseward, and Ben Ridder, and Gregg Afman (in the javelin) qualified for NCAA nationals, where the relay team finished fourth and Afman second.

Working through the possible distraction posed by Calvin's hosting the NCAA Division III national track and field championships in 1977, the squad once again performed nobly. After winning all of their dual meets, the Knights

PEACH COBBLER

Nowadays Calvin's track and field teams spend their spring break training week in waterfront condos on the golden beaches of Gulf Shores, Alabama, competing in pre-season meets with Auburn and Emory universities. It was different in the 1970s. Back then, the men's team loaded school buses, station wagons, and assorted cars to caravan south to the red clay mountains of east Tennessee in search of campgrounds and willing opponents.

We team members didn't especially appreciate our cramped traveling quarters and the nights we spent sleeping in tents as light snow drifted down. But each year we looked forward to Sunday at the rural French Broad Baptist Church, where it had become a tradition that, accompanied by a guitarist from our own ranks, we formed an impromptu choir to sing gospel choruses and old favorites during morning worship.

Our musical offering probably showed more heart than talent, but the reward for our efforts was outstanding. After the service we all trooped to the home of the Ponder family, where we were treated to mountains of delicious Southern food provided by church members, as all semblances of our "training diet" vanished. The peak of this dining nirvana was Mrs. Ponder's homemade peach cobbler. Every member of these teams can taste it still.

Mike Van Denend

combined the strength and experience of veterans with the contributions of new team members to once again claim the MIAA title. Randy Veenstra won the long jump for the third consecutive year, Calvin's sprinters continued to excel, Houseward and Apol dominated the 880, Mike Van Denend finished a sterling second in the mile, and Marvin Rus ran a tough three-mile race. Jack Diemer, Frankie Hiskes, Steve Eckenroth, Jim Busscher, and Dave Vander Kooi all did well in the field events.

The close of the 1977 season also marked the end Dave Tuuk's quarter-century of exemplary service as the coach of track and field. After building the program "from scratch," Tuuk's increasing duties as athletic director now prompted him to place track and field responsibilities in the capable hands of Ralph Honderd.

With its new coach, Calvin continued where it had left off, winning a sixth consecutive league championship. Among the team's mainstays were sprinter Dave Alkema, hurdler John Vander Kamp, and Jon Houseward in the 440 and 880. In the field events the squad was led by pole vaulter Jim Busscher, Ron Cok in the triple jump, and All-MIAA performer Randy Veenstra, who won the long jump for the fourth consecutive year.

The following year, 1979, proved the truth of the adage that "all good things must come to an end," as the Knights stumbled a bit, allowing Albion to win the league title. Veteran team members Cok, Houseward, and Vander Kamp were joined by premier distance runner Doug Diekema as team leaders, but the squad's total effort, though concentrated, fell a bit short.

1980-1989 Steady Pace

Albion won the league championship the next four years, as Calvin consistently placed second. The team's strength was concentrated in cross country runners such as Diekema, John Brink, Kurt Mast, and Mike Kwantes, while Dave Tuuk did well in the middle distances and Jack Hart consistently won points in the shot put. However, the squad lacked the breadth and depth necessary for championship performance.

That situation changed in 1984, however, when Calvin was once again able to mount a solid team effort and regain the MIAA title. Diekema and Kwantes led the distance runners, while Bill Veurink was all-conference in the long jump.

The following two seasons belonged to Hope College with its array of top performers, as Albion and Calvin came in a close second. The Knights' Chris Holstege and Pete Vande Brake constituted a double threat in the hurdle events, Randy Ritsema and Ken DeGraaf led the sprinters, and Todd Vanden Berg was Calvin's main middle distance threat.

As the decade neared its close, a significant development took place in track and field, as a number of specialists joined to assist in coaching various aspects of the sport. Olympian Brian Diemer, now cross country coach, gave invaluable help to Calvin's distance runners on the track team as well. Al Hoekstra, a former distance runner himself, not only joined in helping to coach that aspect of the sport, but also became the ace recruiter for men and women's cross country and track and field. Jim Gardner, a local specialist in the pole vault, volunteered his services as well. These men eventually were joined by other graduates of Calvin's program. This influx of specialty coaches was invaluable in enabling Honderd to put together the kind of team that would dominate MIAA track and field in the 1990s and, under a new head coach, into the new millennium. Only Albion was able to interrupt the Knights' string of championships, and then for only the 1993 season, when it won the title outright, and the 1994 season, when it earned a co-championship with Calvin.

One of the results of this specialization was an increase in outstanding individual performances by a number of Calvin athletes in the late 1980s. Among the track and field athletes who distinguished themselves were John Lumkes and Pat McNamara, the latter winning the national championship in the steeplechase in 1989, and Rick Steenwyk, who excelled in the 800-meter run. Pete Vande Brake became a four-time All-American in the decathlon and was national runner-up in 1987, and pole vaulter Ryan Lubbers was All-MIAA for four consecutive years. Dan Owen was All-American in the high jump three times and was national runner-up in 1987 and 1989. Norm Zylstra exceeded 50 feet in the shot put, as he led in the field events. Of course, the team championships of these years also depended heavily on the unsung heroes who never gained the spotlight, but that does not detract from the individual accomplishments of these exceptional athletes.

1990-2003 A Golden Age

This fifteen-year span was a golden age for the men's track and field program, as a powerful group of athletes led the MIAA in virtually all phases of the sport. John Lumkes was national champion in the steeplechase in 1990. Rick Lubbers, brother of Ryan, was not only an All-MIAA performer for four years but also the national pole vault champion 1991. Robb Steenwyk, an outstanding 800-meter runner, was also a four-time all-conference performer and earned All-American honors three times. David Sydow was a five-time All-American, earning that distinction three times in the 1,500-meter race and twice in the 800 meters. Thad Karnehm, another top distance runner, was named league MVP in 1991 and twice earned All-American status in 5,000 meters and twice in the 10,000 meters. After leaving Calvin, Karnehm qualified for the Olympic trials in 1996.

1995 saw the arrival of J.D. Stein, a transfer from the University of Indiana and an exceptional decathlete who became national champion in 1996. Stein was so versatile that in MIAA meets he could be called to step in for any event in which he was needed. Little wonder that other teams in the MIAA could not match up, as Calvin combined fine individual performances with a balanced team effort.

In 1997, after some 20 years of dedicated, skilled service, Ralph Honderd turned over coaching responsibilities to Jong-Il Kim, a new member of the Physical Education Department. Kim came with solid credentials, having been a long jumper on the South Korean national team and participating in the 1984 and 1988 Olympics. Known for his keen eye for subtle matters of technique, Kim has been able to use that ability to help a number of Calvin's athletes, both men and women.

Among the excellent performers the new coach inherited from Ralph Honderd was John Lumkes' brother Jay, who bolstered the team's middle distance corps by becoming a premier 400-meter runner. During all four years of his Calvin career, from 1996 until 1999, he won All-MIAA status.

Not only did the men's cross country squads of Diemer and Hoekstra totally dominate their MIAA opponents in that sport; they also provided champion distance runners for the track and field team.

Although not a cross country runner, another exceptional athlete came on campus in 1998, the first year of Kim's tenure. Phil Sikkenga proved to be a multi-talented runner who arguably was the greatest sprinter in the history of track and field at Calvin. He set records in the 100-, 200-, and 400-meter sprints, as well as in the 110 high hurdles. In addition, he anchored the 4x100 relay, being nosed out twice in the NCAA national meet, as Calvin's relay team came in second.

The list of athletes gaining All-American status before the turn of the century goes on. In 1998 Geoff Van Dragt was an All-American in the 5,000 meters and the steeplechase; that same year, Steve Michmerhuizen won that distinction in the discus and shot put. Joining Phil Sikkenga the year following were Derek Kleinheksel in the high jump, pole vaulter Mark DeWeerd, and distance runners Dan Hoekstra

Phil Sikkenga

and Lee Doherty. In 1999 the mile relay team of Eric Hansen, Jay Lumkes, Keith Van Goor, and Curt Mulder also received All-American honors.

With the turn of the century, the Calvin track and field team continued to enjoy stunning success, winning four MIAA championships outright. The Knights lost only one dual meet in five years, but even then, the squad completely outclassed the field in the conference meet and thus won a co-championship in 2004.

The parade of All-Americans has continued as well. Van Goor, Hansen, and Steve Abbring joined Sikkenga in receiving that honor in the mile relay in 2000, while Joel Klooster won his award in the 5,000 meters. In 2001 the mile relay team repeated, and they were not alone. High jumpers Cameron Baron and Derek Kleinheksel as well as pole vaulter Mark De Weerd and distance men Hoekstra and Justin Pfruender earned that same distinction.

In 2002 it was Calvin's distance men who dominated the All-American scene: Joel Hoekstra in the 10,000 and 5,000 meters, Justin Pfruender in the steeplechase and 5,000 meters, Hendrik Kok in the 1,500 and 5,000 meters, and Dan Hoekstra in the 5,000 and 10,000 meters. A lone sprinter, Keith Van Goor, also joined that select company. The following year, Nate Meckes won All-American status in the discus and shot put, while the distance corps of Klooster, Kok, and Andy Yazzie also distinguished itself.

The key role of Calvin's remarkable distance crew in the program's earning national recognition cannot be overestimated. In 2002, members of this group placed second, third, sixth, and seventh in the 5,000-meter run, thus propelling Calvin to second place in the final team standings. The performance of a great number of these young men merits the special recognition of distance coaches Brian Diemer and Al Hoekstra, whose work certainly contributed in some measure to Coach Kim's honor of being named NCAA National Division III Men's Coach of the Year in 2003.

WOMEN'S TRACK AND FIELD

1979 A Blazing Start

Women's track and field is a relative newcomer to MIAA competition. Not until 1979 was it inaugurated as a full-fledged league sport. Esther Driesenga was given the challenge of getting Calvin's program underway, and she met it successfully, as the Knights won the title during the first year of the program's existence. Among the members of that first championship squad were Julie Boerman, Sandy Lambers, and Kathy Vander Heide in the short races, Tanis Ryzebol in the 800 and mile run, and Pat Markosky in the two-mile. Field event performers included Kim DeWaard in the shot put, Tanis Ryzebol in the high jump, and Sandy Lambers in the long jump. Women's track and field clearly had gotten off to a strong start at Calvin.

1980-1989 Just Before the Dawn

Both the experience the team had gained during the first year of competition and the addition of incoming athletes paid off in 1980, as Calvin repeated as MIAA champion. The following two years belonged to Hope, yet during that time Driesenga's squad continued to develop and add depth. Calvin's grow-

ing strength was due in large measure to the contributions of the following women: Sue Maat and Flo Slomp in the javelin, Janice Weeber in the discus, Kathy Haun in the 800, and Tara deVries in the 3,000 meters. The Knights also continued to dominate in the two relay events.

Thus it was no surprise when Calvin once again won the MIAA championship in 1983. In addition to that achievement, the team also qualified its first athletes for participation in the NCAA Division III track and field meet, and they competed successfully, as the 400-meter relay team, composed of Sue Schaafsma, Lisa De Young, Judy Meyer, and Kim Lautenbach, placed fourth in the nation. During the regular season Kim Lautenbach and Lisa DeYoung controlled the short races, while Lori Dubois added strength in the high jump.

1984 saw Calvin win the league championship once again. The strong performance of three team members, in particular, contributed significantly to the squad's success, as Barb Zoodsma and Dawn Walstrom strengthened the short races, and versatile Laura Vroon, doubling in softball and track and field, was champion in the 3,000 meters. Vroon supplemented her regular season success that same year

TRAVELING MERCIES

In the early days of competition, Calvin's teams usually traveled to away contests by car. The coach, and sometimes responsible students, would usually drive, with faculty members from other departments occasionally helping out. As time went on, the department began to use twelve-passenger vans to transport men's and women's teams, and to rent buses when a large number of athletes were involved. The number of miles that Calvin teams traveled in all those years had to be in the hundreds of thousands. More recently, teams have been afforded the luxury of traveling by air-conditioned coach, or even by plane, when the destination is on either the east or west coast.

In all of those travels, never once did any team or individual incur serious accident or injury. For this we give praise to our Almighty God for his care and keeping. Psalm 91:11 reads, "For he will command his angels concerning you, to guard you in all your ways."

by attaining All-American status in the 5,000 meters in the NCAA championships.

The following five years saw struggle and change. Calvin fell back, as Hope and Alma fielded particularly strong teams. So much for the struggle. The change involved the team's coaches, as Mary Jo Louters replaced Driesenga for 1987 and 1988, and Gregg Afman took Louters' place in 1989.

Despite the lean years that the squad experienced over the last half of the decade, several Calvin athletes stood out. Donna VanderVeen excelled in the discus, as did Kristin Hiemstra and Grace Slomp in the javelin and Tammy Oostendorp in the 200 and 400 meters. In addition, the Knights consistently produced quality relay teams that either won or placed high in both the 4x100 and 4x400 races.

When Afman, a former three-time All-American javelin thrower for Calvin, assumed coaching responsibilities in 1989, Alma still held the top spot in the conference. However, a "golden age" in women's track and field was about to dawn for the Knights.

1990-2003 Sweeping with a Broad Broom

As the new decade began, Coach Afman organized a new system that utilized the skills of specialty coaches. Al Hoekstra and Brian Diemer used their expertise to help train distance runners, as did Robert Hyde, a graduate of the men's cross country program. Steve Seth, an All-American javelin thrower, gave assistance in that event, and Norm Zylstra coached women in the discus and shot put. Jim Gardner, in addition to coaching the pole vaulters on the men's squad, also gave tips to the women competing in that event. Kathy Haddox, a three-time All-American, assisted as well.

As was the case in the men's program, here, too, the remarkable success of the women's cross country program, which has won 15 consecutive MIAA championships, also has contributed richly to the success of track and field at Calvin.

Already in 1990 the results of the new system began to surface. Not only did the Knights handily win the league title, but they also sent a strong representation to the NCAA championships. At that meet Kelli Lautenbach placed fourth in the 400-meter dash, Lisa Visbeen took third in the javelin, and the Knights' mile relay team, composed of Kelli Lautenbach, Denise Griffioen, Julie Bos, and Gretchen Toxopeus, placed eighth in its event. At the close of the season, Lautenbach was named league MVP, the first Calvin female athlete to win that distinction in track and field.

As the years passed, Calvin's string of consecutive championships in women's track and field continued to lengthen, as each year the Knights won the MIAA title. They also continued to send representatives to the NCAA championships.

In 1991 Calvin placed 18th nationally on the basis of Kelli Lautenbach-Schutte's seventh place in the 400-meter dash and Lisa Visbeen's eighth-place showing in the javelin. Though scoring only nine points in 1992, the Knights did send two relay teams to the national meet. Shawn Farmer, Tammy Vander Ploeg, Melissa Dykstra, and Kathy Haddox ran the 4x400 race, while Angie Feinauer, Shawn Farmer, Kathy Haddox, and Patsy Orkar represented Calvin in the 400-meter relay.

Kelli Lautenbach

The 1993 national meet saw Afman's squad move forward to a fourth-place NCAA finish, with 41 points. Angie Feinauer became national champion in the long jump, and she also participated with Orkar, Haddox, and Farmer in the winning 4x100 relay. In addition, Kendra Douma placed third in the javelin, Renea Bluekamp took fourth in the 10,000 meters and fifth in the 5,000 meters, Becky Kuntzleman came in fifth in the heptathlon, and Haddox ran eighth in the 100-meter dash.

The following year, Calvin moved up yet another notch, finishing in a remarkable third place nationally. Contributing to this fine achievement were several athletes. The 1,600-meter relay team of Farmer, Haddox, Holly Breuker, and Melissa Dykstra won its event; Renea Bluekamp once again doubled, placing second in the 10,000 meters and third in the 5,000 meters; Amy Kuipers, also running in two events, took fifth in the 10,000 meters and seventh in the 5,000 meters; Breuker came in fifth in the 400-meter hurdles; Esther Vahrmeyer was a sixth-place finisher in the heptathlon; and Kendra Douma placed eighth in the javelin.

The 1995 squad could not duplicate the exceptional performance of its forerunner, but it did place twelfth nationally. In the distances, Betsy Haverkamp ran third in the 5,000-meter run, and Renea Bluekamp took fourth in the 10,000 meters, the same race in which Amy Kuipers placed eighth. Holly Breuker finished fourth in the 400-meter hurdles, while high jumper Gwen Erffmeyer took eighth in her event.

Calvin's women placed seventh nationally the next two years. Breuker was champion in the 400-meter hurdles in 1996, while Amy Kuipers improved her performance of the previous season by placing fifth in both the 5,000 and 10,000 meters. Rounding out the team's effort was Jennifer Rottschafer, who finished sixth in the 400-meter hurdles; and Esther Vahrmeyer, who won points in the hepthathlon. In 1997 Betsy Haverkamp ran superbly, taking first place in the 3,000-meter run and second in the 5,000 meters, while Jennifer Rottschafer moved up to third in the 400-meter hurdles, and Lisa Timmer placed seventh in the 3,000-meter run.

The 1998 squad dropped to 11th place in the national meet, but two Knights won All-American honors for the second year in a row: Jennifer Rottschafer again took third place in the 400-meter hurdles, and Lisa Timmer moved up a notch to sixth place in the 3,000 meters. In addition, Megan Pierce finished sixth in the 400-meter dash, while Calvin's 4x400 meter relay team of Rottschafer, Pierce, Kristi Van Woerkom, and Sarah Veltkamp finished a strong third. Andrea Clark, Timmer's colleague as a distance runner, also gained All-American status, taking eighth place in the 10,000-meter run.

Calvin was once again exceptionally strong in 1999, finishing fourth in the national meet. Megan Pierce led the team with a first-place performance in the 400-meter dash, moving up from sixth the year before. In the distance races, Sarah Gritter performed well, placing second in the 3,000-meter run and third in the 1,500. Lindsay Mulder finished fourth in the long jump, while Calvin's 4x400 relay unit, consisting of Veltkamp, Van Woerkom, Pierce, and Mulder, distinguished itself by winning the national championship.

The 1999 season marked the close of Gregg Afman's tenure as coach of women's track and field, as he left to take a position at Westmont College in California. Under his leadership, Calvin's women won 10 consecutive MIAA championships and performed consistently well at the national level. While gratefully acknowledging the exceptional efforts of the many All-Americans gracing his teams, Afman also stresses that many other fine, dedicated athletes were vital to the team's total performance and deserve respect, even though space limitations will not allow for their recognition as individuals within the context of this volume.

Ralph Honderd came back to coach the Knights for the next two seasons, as the team's success continued. The squad placed fifth in the NCAA championship in 2000, with Megan Pierce becoming national champion in the 400-meter dash and running one leg for the victorious 4x400 team composed of Pierce, Lindsay Mulder, Veltkamp, and Mindy Worst. In addition, Sarah Gritter came in fourth in the 3,000 meters, and Lindsay Mulder finished in the same position in the long jump.

Calvin's second-place NCAA finish in 2001 was the highest it had earned to that point. Contributing to that excellent result were the efforts of a number of fine athletes. Lindsay Mulder moved from the fourth place she won in 2000 to claim the long jump title, participating as well in the repeat championship earned by the 4x400 meter team. Megan Pierce was runner-up in the 400-meter dash; Rachel Veltkamp took third in the pole vault; Annie Vander Laan, fourth in the heptathlon; Andrea Rip, seventh in the javelin; and the versatile Lindsay Mulder, seventh in the 400-meter dash. Honderd's stint with the women's squad was short but eminently satisfying.

In 2002 Jong-Il Kim took over as head coach for both the men's and women's track and field teams, the first time Calvin employed a full-time person to coach the sport. The three women's teams he has coached have seen excellent success. In 2002 Kim's squad placed 12th nationally. Annie Vander Laan repeated her fourth-place heptathlon finish of 2001, while Katie Corner took fifth in the discus. Both relay teams also did well, with the 4x100 unit—which included Veltkamp, Vander Laan, Worst, and Sue Abbring—finishing fifth, and the 4x400 squad—made up of Worst, Vander Laan, Veltkamp and Abbring—finishing seventh.

Rachel Veltkamp

Calvin's 2003 squad moved up to sixth place. Although only Annie Vander Laan won an individual championship, and that in the heptathlon, a number of additional athletes finished high in their events, resulting in a total of 30 team points. Katie Corner improved to second place in the discus, Jessie Lair placed 15th in the 1,000-meter run, Vander Laan was sixth in the 100-meter hurdles, and Christine Hendricks came in eighth in the heptathlon. Sarah Hastings earned points in two events, finishing 14th in the 3,000-meter steeplechase and 12th in the 5,000-meter run. Rounding out Calvin's effort were Laura Hamilton, ninth-place finisher in the 400-meter hurdles; Sue Abbring, who came in fourth in the 200-meter dash; and the 4x100 relay team of Abbring, Hamilton, Vander Laan, and Kristen Carlson, which took fourth place.

Given the unusually consistent performance by Calvin's women, it was no surprise that Coach Kim was named National Coach of the Year for women's track and field in both 2002 and 2003. The 2003 honor, coupled with the same men's track and field national recognition, represented the first time one coach received both the men's and women's National Coach of the Year award.

WOMEN'S VOLLEYBALL

1965-1969 Serving Up a New Sport

With the new Fieldhouse a reality, volleyball emerged as another athletic activity in which Calvin women were interested. During these early years there was no league structure for the sport. As a result, the team played any competition available, including large universities such as Western Michigan and Michigan State. Karen Timmer, an accomplished athlete during her years as a student at Calvin, was one of the first coaches. The squad included two units, I and II, both of which played at various play days involving a number of schools.

1970-1979 Digging Deep

In 1972 volleyball became a championship sport in the WMIAA. Calvin's team, coached by Annlies Knoppers, won the first league title. The following year, three very talented athletes—Kathy De Boer, Diane Spoelstra, and Laurie Zoodsma—led the team to another championship. Knoppers then left Calvin to join the staff at Michigan State University, and this gifted trio decided to follow her. The loss of these remarkable athletes was doubly difficult for Calvin, since all

three of them also played basketball.

Knoppers was replaced on the Calvin staff by Karla Hoesch, who had been an accomplished athlete at Hope College. After a year of teaching at the elementary school level, she was eager to become volleyball and softball coach at Calvin, serving for one year also as women's basketball coach. (During that season, 1978-79, while Hoesch worked with the basketball team, Nancy Van Noord filled in as volleyball coach.)

Two changes took place in 1978, as the decade neared its close. First, volleyball became a championship sport in the MIAA, which had just expanded to include women's athletics, and second, Calvin's dominance came to a temporary end, as Adrian developed a series of outstanding teams. The early years of Calvin's program had been productive, however, and helped establish a strong volleyball tradition.

1980-1989 A Spike Up in Achievement

Adrian's brief run of MIAA championships ended after 1981. In the 1982-83 season Coach Karla Hoesch Wolters' Knights earned a co-championship, sharing the title with Alma. The same year, the first time that the league selected an MVP, Deb

GRACE AT THE TOP

The 1986 Division III volleyball finals held at Calvin made a deep impression on both players and fans. Roxane Helmus Steenhuysen, a member of that team, recalls even today the thrill of playing before 3,500 fans and the remarkable support of the Calvin staff, student body, and alumni.

Like Steenhuysen, teammate Julie Dykstra Tiesman remembers "the energy in that packed gym." Although losing the fifth game after being up 2-1 was "really tough," it has given her "special empathy for teams that lose in the 'big game.'" Despite the loss, Tiesman says even today that she "wouldn't have missed it for the world."

Texas native Leah Calsbeek Schipper, another volleyball player that year, remembers it as a "season of dreams." She, too, recalls the heartbreak of that final loss to the University of California–San Diego, but is able to see God's hand "not only in the good times, but also when we lost. He gave us the ability," Schipper gratefully remembers, "to find joy in happy moments, but also grace in defeat."

Although the following year, 1985, resulted in an undefeated MIAA season and a win in the NCAA regionals, 1986 proved to be a more signal season in the history of Calvin volleyball. After completing its league schedule without a loss, Wolters' team moved successfully through the first stages of the NCAA tournament, defeating in turn Buffalo, Ohio Northern, and Wisconsin–LaCrosse. Calvin was then granted the honor of hosting the national final game against California–San Diego.

Over 3,500 spectators, the largest crowd in NCAA Division III volleyball history, showed up for this championship match-up. The Knights lost the first game but then came back strong to win the next two. San Diego then evened the match with a fourth-game victory, forcing a "rubber game" to determine who would win the national title. Calvin's partisan fans were disappointed, as their favorites fell 15-5, but they were cheered by their team's splendid achievement, a

Julie Dykstra   **Leah Calsbeek**   **Roxane Helmus**

VerHill received that honor. With strong leadership by veteran Lynn Bolt, the team also performed very well in 1984. Though coming in second to a strong Alma team during the regular season, Calvin upset the Scots in NCAA regional tournament play. Coach Wolters' crew followed that victory with wins over Ohio Northern and North Carolina–Greensboro before losing in the Final Four, first to MIT and then to La Verne (California). Nevertheless, that fourth-place national finish represented a fine achievement by the team of 1984.

second-place finish in the national finals. Wolters was named Division III Volleyball Coach of the Year, and three of her athletes—Julie Dykstra, Leah Calsbeek, and Roxane Helmus—earned All-American honors.

At the conclusion of this outstanding season, Coach Wolters accepted the invitation of her alma mater, Hope College, to coach on its staff. Wolters spent 13 years at Calvin, primarily as softball and volleyball coach, and was instrumental in significantly raising the level of play in both sports.

Janna Ter Molen, who had been on some of Calvin's championship teams in the early 1980s, was then chosen to take over the volleyball program. Hope College won the MIAA title in 1987, Ter Molen's first year of coaching, but Calvin earned the league championship in both 1988 and 1989, with Amber Blankespoor winning MVP recognition both seasons. Although Ohio Northern defeated Calvin in NCAA tournament play both years, the decade had been deeply satisfying.

1990-2003 Digs, Blocks, and Kills

Calvin's fine play continued in 1990, as the squad once again qualified for post-season competition, defeating Allegheny College but then losing to Washington University (Missouri). It was at this juncture that Coach Ter Molen decided to go on to graduate school in pursuit of her doctorate.

Ter Molen's successor, Mary Schutten, came to Calvin with excellent credentials. As the very successful head volleyball coach at Dordt College, she had gained considerable experience and had developed keen coaching and leadership skills. Her first year at Calvin saw Kalamazoo win the league title, but in 1992 her squad went undefeated in the MIAA and finished in fourth place nationally in the NCAA tournament, defeating Baldwin-Wallace and Thomas More (Kentucky) before losing to Washington University. The play of three seniors was vital to this splendid effort: middle hitters Pam Van Tol and Christy Veltman and setter Betsy Wilgenburg. Wilgenburg was honored by being voted league MVP for the season. The following year the team was also successful, tying Kalamazoo College for the MIAA title.

SPUNK

In 1997 a spunky Calvin volleyball team was playing in the MIAA regional tournament. Having defeated Muskingum College in three games, the Knights came up against Wittenberg, the top-ranked team in the nation. After dropping the first two games, Calvin rallied for three straight wins, 15-13, 15-10, and 15-10, thus upsetting the top team in the region. Even though her team then lost to Ohio Northern, Coach Schutten considered the win over Wittenberg one of the greatest victories in the history of Calvin women's volleyball.

Kalamazoo and Hope were dominant the next five years, with Calvin always finishing near the top in the MIAA standings. Coach Schutten's squad continued to be blessed with gifted players, among them Erika Van Stralen, Erin Hall, and Kristine Den Hollander, who was voted league MVP in 1996. In 1999 Calvin broke through to win the MIAA championship again; the play of Charla Holmes and Rhonda Volkers, who was voted MVP in both 1999 and 2000, was a major factor in that year's success. After the 2000 season Volkers was also honored by being given All-American recognition.

At the conclusion of the 2000 season, Coach Schutten decided to move on to a position at Western Michigan University. Her tenure at Calvin had been very successful, with her teams qualifying five times for the NCAA national tournament.

For the 2001 season Jerry Bergsma served as interim coach. His team did very well, compiling a 22-12 overall record. Although finishing third in the league, the squad won the conference championship by defeating Hope in the title match, thereby earning an automatic berth in the Division III tournament. Although the Knights were defeated in the first round of play by nationally ranked Carnegie-Mellon, their season had been a solid success.

Amber Blankespoor Warners was appointed Schutten's successor in 2002 and has done an excellent job of maintaining Calvin's strong volleyball tradition. Coach Warners brought extensive playing experience to her new position. Included in her background was membership on the Calvin team that took second place nationally in 1986. Under her leadership, Calvin finished high in the quest for the MIAA title in 2002, losing out only to Kalamazoo. Trisha Balkema, Melissa Pell, and Laura Tucker were three of the team's principal players that year.

In 2003 Calvin's squad reached the 20-win mark for the ninth straight year, posting a 28-8 overall record and finishing second in the league, falling to Alma in the conference tournament. Balkema, Kara Kuipers, and Kristen Kalb made outstanding contributions during this second year of Warners' tenure as coach.

Looking to the future, Calvin fans have every reason to anticipate a continuation of the fine play that has consistently marked the program.

WRESTLING

1969-1982 On the Mat

Wrestling was new to Calvin College when the MIAA voted to include it in the list of men's activities in 1969. It is a sport for the hale and hearty, with no room for the timid or faint-hearted. It takes strength and strategy to achieve a final takedown and pin. While winning a wrestling match is a great personal sensation, there usually are no large crowds to add glory to such a victory. And if one loses, one also bears that loss alone.

Selected to direct Calvin's first team in 1969 was Jim Webster, wrestling coach at Creston High School in Grand Rapids. Few students expressed interest in the program, but one who did was Dick Vliem, who remained undefeated during the 1969 season and was voted the league's most valuable wrestler at the conclusion of this first year of MIAA competition.

Calvin men lost more matches than they won the following year, finishing fifth in the league. For the second time, Dick Vliem did not lose a match in MIAA competition. Others placing high were Dan Holesinger, who finished second, and Randy Commeret, who took fifth place.

1971 was another year of struggle. Dick Vliem, Calvin's ace during the previous two seasons, had transferred. Remaining on the team were only eight wrestlers: Ted Boersma, Ken Langerak, Jake Van Wyk, Jim Breuker, Gaylen "Butch" Byker, and seniors Randy Commeret, Ed Bos, and Dick Lyzenga. Coach Webster was correct in asserting that the key to wrestling's future success at Calvin lay in stimulating interest in the sport on the part of students. That interest, however, did not seem forthcoming.

In 1972 Neil Starks became Calvin's coach. Starks had been an all-state wrestler in high school and had coached for a number of years in the Grandville school system. Though Starks was optimistic at the

Dick Vliem

outset, his hopes were not immediately realized. Calvin finished in the lower half of the MIAA during his first year, even though Cal Van Reken, Ted Boersma, and "Butch" Byker each had a pin. As in the past, spectator attendance at home meets was very poor.

Tom Ten Brink

Coach Starks' 1973 team included several returnees. Contributing to a fourth-place league finish were Tom Ten Brink, Ted Boersma, Jake Van Wyk, Cal Van Reken, Ken Langerak, and Davey Smith. Crucial to that finish was a 35½-30 win over Hope.

1974 proved to be the best year ever for Calvin wrestling. A crowd of over 100 watched while Calvin routed a visiting "B" squad from Notre Dame by a 32-12 score. This outstanding performance was followed by a victory over archrival Hope. In the Hope meet, Cal Van Reken registered his eighth pin of the season, an accomplishment that helped Calvin significantly in its 30-6 triumph. Calvin's only loss in league play was to Olivet. The Knights appeared to have become a force to be reckoned with in MIAA wrestling.

In the conference meet Calvin was the only team to give Olivet any real competition, scoring 97 points to the 148 won by Olivet. Scott Yerrick and Tom Ten Brink won their weight classes, and both were named to the All-MIAA team. Four Calvin wrestlers gave outstanding second-place performances: Ted Boersma, Davy Smith, Cal Van Reken, and Pat Sherman. Starks was proud of his team's second-place finish and hoped that a winning tradition had begun to emerge.

However, optimism did not reign for long. Team members were notified before the following season began that Coach Starks had accepted a job with the Peninsular Club

in downtown Grand Rapids. Disappointed, several members left the team. Ed Bos, a former Calvin wrestler, coached the squad through the tough 1975 season. Bright spots were few and far between, but Tom Ten Brink did win his weight class and was named All-MIAA for the third-straight year. Rich Van Dyken, Pat Sherman, Andy Wunderink, and Rich Westman persevered throughout the season, but despite the best efforts of these five wrestlers, Calvin's 1975 team only faintly resembled the 1974 squad. For the next three years, Calvin did not even have a wrestling team.

Jeff Pettinga, who had had some experience as a wrestling coach at Grand Rapids Christian High School, made an attempt to revive the program for the 1978-79 season. Thirteen wrestlers made up the squad, but, according to Pettinga, 70 percent of them had no prior experience. As a result, Calvin completed the season with four wins, eight losses, and one tie, finishing last in the MIAA. Highlights of the year were the 10-7 record of Scott Glass and a 27-24 victory over Hope.

The following year, 1979, John Beck was hired as coach. Like Pettinga, he had coached wrestling in high school. Though Calvin placed second in the Christian College Meet, three weight classes remained unfilled, which meant that Calvin started each meet at an obvious disadvantage. In the MIAA championships, Calvin finished in sixth place, and in dual meets they finished fifth, which netted them an overall fifth place in the final league standings. Scott Glass and Tom Kool did their bit by providing better than average performances.

The coaching parade continued in 1980-81. Tom Ten Brink, who had been an All-MIAA Calvin wrestler in the 1970s, was appointed as Coach Beck's successor. His hopes for a successful season were partially realized when, in spite of injuries, Calvin placed first in the Christian College Meet. Gaining pins were John Lubben and Tom Kool. Taking second were Scott Glass, David Shier, and Jeff Clousing. In the MIAA conference meet, Tom Kool was a first-place winner and was voted All-MIAA. Though qualifying for nationals, Kool lost a hard-fought match to the number-one seed in his weight class. Since the year had seen a measure of success, "wait and see" were the hopeful watchwords with which the team contemplated the next year.

Ten Brink was unable to return as coach for the 1981-82 season, however. Once again, Jeff Pettinga tried valiantly to keep the sport alive. Few athletes came out for the team; as a consequence, Calvin finished last in the MIAA. Despite the difficult season, Pettinga had high praise for senior Scott Glass and juniors Todd Groenhout and Tom Kool for their leadership and consistent winning efforts.

Although a few league schools continued competing, the MIAA dropped wrestling at the close of the 1981-82 season. Its demise was not long lamented at Calvin. Spectator interest over the years had been minimal. As a result, notes Pettinga, motivation had to come purely from within each wrestler. In the absence of a pattern of success, such motivation was difficult to generate on a consistent level. In any case, after some 10 years of MIAA competition, wrestling at Calvin was no more.

PART TWO

STORIES AND STATISTICS

1953-2003

SIGNIFICANT MILESTONES FOR CALVIN COLLEGE IN THE MIAA

1953   Calvin is admitted to the MIAA and WMIAA.

1965   MIAA institutes MVP awards; first recipient, in golf, is Dave Tuls.

1968   Field hockey becomes a WMIAA sport.

1969   Wrestling becomes an MIAA championship sport.

1970   Heavyweight Dick Vliem of Calvin becomes the first recipient of the league's Most Valuable Wrestler award.

1971   Men's soccer becomes an MIAA championship sport in the fall; Calvin and Hope are co-champs.

1972   Men's swimming becomes an MIAA championship sport (1970-71).

1973   Men's golf is moved to the fall; volleyball becomes a WMIAA championship sport.

1974   Women's basketball becomes a WMIAA championship sport (1972-73).

1976   MIAA college presidents approve post-season competition.

1977   Women's swimming and softball become WMIAA championship sports.

Presidents of MIAA colleges approve combined governance of men's and women's sports.

Mark Veenstra (basketball) is the first athlete in MIAA history to be voted the league's Most Valuable Player four years in succession.

1978   The MIAA and WMIAA are combined to form a unified men's and women's league; 1978-79 is the first year of this new system.

1979   Women's track and field becomes an MIAA championship sport; Calvin is the first champion. Calvin is also the first MIAA softball champion.

1981   Women's archery is dropped as a championship sport; women's cross country becomes an MIAA championship sport.

1982   Wrestling is dropped as an MIAA championship sport.

League All-Sports Awards are determined for the first time on the basis of both men's and women's sports.

All-Conference and Most Valuable Player recognition are first given in women's sports; Sharon Boeve of Calvin is MVP in both basketball and softball; Deb VerHill wins the award in volleyball.

1988   The MIAA, America's oldest collegiate conference, commemorates its 100th year of continuous operation.

1989   Soccer becomes an MIAA championship sport for women.

1990   Field hockey has its final year of competition, due to an inadequate number of teams in the league; women's soccer takes its place.

1991   Women's golf becomes an MIAA championship sport.

Rick Lubbers is national champion in the pole vault.

1992   Calvin is NCAA Division III basketball champion, and Ed Douma is named Division III National Coach of the Year.

1993   The first post-season women's basketball tournament is held to determine the league's qualifier for the NCAA Division III playoffs; Calvin is the first tournament champion.

Renea Bluekamp of Calvin wins the women's NCAA Division III cross country championship. She becomes the first MIAA athlete, male or female, to win the gold medal in a national cross country meet.

1995   The Calvin women qualify for the NCAA Division III playoffs in softball.

Amy Kuipers becomes the first MIAA female athlete to achieve NCAA Division III All-American honors for four consecutive years in cross country. In spring 1996 she becomes Calvin's first female athlete to win All-MIAA honors eight times in her career.

1997   A new NCAA Division III men's basketball attendance record is established as 11,442 fans watch Calvin play Hope at the Van Andel Arena in Grand Rapids.

1998   The women's cross country team wins the NCAA Division III national championship.

1999   For the first time, the MIAA qualifies three teams for the NCAA championship in women's soccer; Calvin is one of those teams.

Calvin repeats as NCAA Division III women's cross country champions.

2000   Calvin becomes the first MIAA college to win two NCAA Division III national team championships in a school year (1999-2000): in women's cross country and men's basketball.

In the fall, Calvin's men's team captures the NCAA Division III national championship in cross country, a first for the MIAA.

2001   The Calvin College women's track 1600-meter relay wins the NCAA Division III national championship for a third consecutive year. Members of the relay are Lindsay Mulder, Megan Pierce, Sara Veltkamp, and Mindy Worst.

2002   For the first time in league history, the MIAA has three teams finish in the top ten at the NCAA Division III men's swimming and diving championships, with Hope coming in fifth, Kalamazoo sixth, and Calvin ninth.

Calvin has four All-American performances in the men's 5,000-meter, which marks the first time in NCAA track and field championship history that four runners from the same school achieve All-American distinction in the event: Joel Klooster comes in second, Hendrik Kok third, Justin Pfruender sixth, and Dan Hoekstra seventh.

2003   The men's cross country team wins another NCAA Division III national championship.

A BRIEF GLOSSARY OF TERMS FOR WOMEN'S ATHLETICS

AIAW—Association of Intercollegiate Athletics for Women

> When federal authorities passed Title IX, which gave women equal opportunity in the area of sports, the AIAW was founded, a national organization that regulated women's sports, sponsored championship events, and the like.

SMAIAW—State of Michigan Association of Intercollegiate Athletics for Women

> The SMAIAW was the state-level organization of the AIAW and performed for Michigan colleges and universities functions similar to those of the national organization. Calvin's Doris Zuidema played an influential role in the development and governance of the SMAIAW. Her teams competed favorably under the SMAIAW, winning numerous state championships.

MAIAW—Midwest Association of Intercollegiate Athletics for Women

> The MAIAW functioned as the regional body between the SMAIAW and the AIAW.

After a number of years of foot-dragging, the NCAA came to its senses and decided to include women in its powerful organization.

VOICES FROM THE MIAA
AND ITS MEMBER COLLEGES

From MIAA Commissioner David L. Neilson

Calvin College joined the MIAA in 1953 and has contributed greatly to the success and heritage of our conference—the oldest athletic conference in the United States. It is my opinion that Calvin has positively influenced the MIAA in several critical ways. First, its coaching and athletic administration have shown high ethical standards consistent with the mission of the MIAA. Second, Calvin's teams and individual athletes are highly competitive on both the MIAA and NCAA level. And third, both the men's and women's programs at Calvin consistently demonstrate that it is possible to meld academic and athletic success on the college level.

We look forward to the next 50 years of Calvin College's membership in our conference and fully expect their legacy of athletic achievement and outstanding student-athletes to continue.

> *David L. Neilson*
> *Commissioner, Michigan Intercollegiate*
> *Athletic Association*

From former MIAA Commissioner Albert Deal

Calvin's entry as a member institution of the MIAA was a positive development, both for the college and the league.

When Calvin entered in 1953, the MIAA had been in operation for 65 years. In that period the league had survived the Spanish-American War, World Wars I and II, and countless other threatening incidents—among them financial depressions and changes in institutional memberships.

At some point, each MIAA member institution could claim a relationship or identity with a Protestant Christian church. Some of those ties were very close; others were obscure. The influence of the Christian Reformed Church on the program and operation of Calvin College was unmistakable. That influence has not infringed upon or disrupted in any way the operation of the MIAA.

During its years of membership in the MIAA Calvin College has experienced outstanding leadership in the administration of its athletic program. Among those leaders were Dr. John DeVries, Calvin's first faculty representative on the MIAA Board of Governors, and Barney Steen, David Tuuk, Don Vroon, Marvin Zuidema, and Ralph Honderd. During the past half-century Calvin coaches have had the opportunity to direct many outstanding student-athletes.

It has been very interesting for me to observe the role Calvin College has played as a member of the oldest intercollegiate athletic conference in the United States.

> *Albert L. Deal*
> *MIAA Commissioner, 1971-1979*

From Joseph Cooper, MIAA Supervisor of Officials

I began my contacts with Calvin College as an official when games were played at Burton Gym, the Civic Auditorium, and Grand Rapids Christian High School. My great memories of Calvin began back then and extend to the present. After serving as an official, I advanced to my present position as the MIAA's supervisor of officials.

Several observations in my experience with Calvin continue to impress me. The first is the first-class sportsmanship that the coaches, players, and fans show. The second is the

106

fact that administration of Calvin games is beyond reproach. The third is that, before home games at Calvin, all concerned actually sing "The Star Spangled Banner." And finally, I always feel welcome at Calvin. Thus it was no problem when, for the last Calvin game I worked, I actually had to come out of the stands as a replacement for a missing official!

Joseph R. Cooper
MIAA Supervisor of Officials

From Adrian College

When I reflect on women's athletic competition between Adrian College and Calvin in the 1960s, 1970s, and early 1980s, intense rivalry and exceptional sportsmanship come to mind. Title IX may have changed women's programs at large universities, but prior to that, Calvin was a leader in the WMIAA (Women's Michigan Intercollegiate Athletic Association) and state organizations. The value of women competing was an important part of Calvin's philosophy and was reinforced by dedicated coaches.

Playing on the road against Calvin was memorable, as large crowds supported the women, unheard of at other away sites. And if you managed a victory, it seemed like a national championship was won.

My respect for Calvin in the WMIAA and MIAA began in 1964 and still continues, as I watch current competition.

Nancy Walsh
Head Basketball Coach

I logged some 30 years as coach and look back on my associations with the MIAA and Calvin College with a great deal of respect. I coached a number of sports for Adrian College, and competition with Calvin was always intense and demanded a high level of play on our part. Calvin's program was characterized by good athletes and excellent coaching, a combination which always made them a formidable opponent.

Gregg Arbaugh
Athletic Director; Golf, Cross Country,
Baseball, Tennis, and Basketball Coach

From Albion College

Calvin College epitomizes the best in Division III athletics. Their athletes were truly students who were intent on becoming doctors, lawyers, and career professionals in many fields. Calvin became a beacon of light in formulating the philosophy and mission of the MIAA.

Though fiercely competitive, Calvin brought a sense of integrity and dignity to the arena. At Albion, defeating a Calvin team often highlighted our season. Our rivalry was intense, our respect even greater.

The Steens and the Tuuks made Calvin proud.

Elkin Isaac
Athletic Director, Track and Field Coach

After Calvin College joined the MIAA, its fine athletic programs increased opportunities for both male and female students in all the MIAA colleges to participate in athletic events at a higher competitive level.

Special thanks to Doris Zuidema for her leadership in the WMIAA/MIAA and AIAW/NCAA. She promoted high levels of skill, good sportsmanship, and equal opportunities for all in athletics. One cannot think of Doris without congratulating her for her many years of coaching a variety of sports teams to many MIAA championships.

May the many fine relationships between the students and coaches of Albion and Calvin and the other MIAA colleges continue indefinitely.

Char Duff
Women's Athletic Director and Coach

From Alma College

I recall that the ageless one, Barney Steen, circulated a lengthy questionnaire in the later 1960s, requesting feedback that would assist a probative committee of faculty and staff in recommending whether "Calvin College should institute football as a competitive sport." The Alma coaches were extremely grateful when the group decided not to introduce football. Victories in other sports were scarce enough.

In the early 1960s the Calvin staff also made available to us the planning document used in the development of the new physical education and recreation center on the Knollcrest campus. This guide was especially helpful in developing the new physical education center at Alma, which we dedicated in 1968. The generosity of the Calvin staff in sharing planning details and a building-use philosophy assisted our staff immeasurably. For me, this act typified the MIAA spirit of cooperation within a competitive environment.

Charlie Gray
Director of Athletics,
Track and Cross Country Coach

From Hope College

For a variety of reasons, Calvin College was a natural for MIAA membership in 1953. Its academic tradition was well established, and it enjoyed stability through its close association with the Christian Reformed Church. Calvin's endorsement of the student-athlete, in that order, was in keeping with MIAA philosophy. Hope College athletes were well aware of Calvin's quality athletic teams and now looked forward to an added dimension in the fabled Hope-Calvin rivalry.

In its 50-year membership, Calvin has won its share of league titles, has hosted national championships in basketball and track, and has won NCAA championships in basketball and cross country. The MIAA can well be proud of these accomplishments.

Gordon Brewer
Director of Athletics,
Track and Cross Country Coach

In the 1970s Calvin College, with its larger student population, was the dominant force in most WMIAA women's sports. Hope College women always tried hard to measure up to Calvin women, due to the strong rivalry between the men's programs. Hope women would strive to give Calvin women a good game, but would fall short of victory.

Somewhere in the late 1970s or early 1980s the women athletic directors at Hope and Calvin decided that the two colleges would share a bus to Northern Michigan University to compete at a field hockey tournament. Both Doris Zuidema and I were field hockey coaches at our schools. Many at both schools were in disbelief [convinced that, due to our rivalries, such an arrangement would never work]. On the long trip to Marquette, Hope got on the bus first and claimed the back seats. Calvin occupied the front. Doris and I wondered if we had made a mistake. However, on the way home two days later, many Hope and Calvin players were sharing seats and enjoying new friendships.

Over the years, Calvin and Hope have become the dominant programs for women in the MIAA. The two programs will always be competitive with one another, due to the many commonalities they share and the respect they have for each other.

Anne Irwin
Women's Athletic Director

For myself, I was much for Calvin's [entering the MIAA]. It was a rivalry, all right. However, I knew that Calvin would be competing on equal terms as far as philosophy of sport was concerned. From experiences coaching against Calvin in basketball and track, I had gained respect for their coaches and players.

[Calvin's admittance to the MIAA] proved to be, for Hope, a good move. We had an intense rivalry that included practically all sports. Mention Calvin to Hope athletes, and we would be fired up! Also, on most issues of substance in the MIAA, Hope and Calvin would see eye to eye. This was due to the similarities of the schools and the meaning of sport in both athletic departments.

Calvin's being in the MIAA has made, at least for Hope, championships more meaningful. It meant we had beaten them!

For myself, as a coach, playing Calvin meant I was coaching against a friend. What is more fun than beating an equal!

Russ DeVette
Basketball and Track Coach

From Kalamazoo College

In the course of my 32 years at Kalamazoo College I enjoyed competing against and working with the athletic administrators and coaches at Calvin College. I had a wonderful personal and professional relationship with them that I treasure still today. I held these men and women in high esteem for their concern for establishing an environment for fair and equitable competition in the league. Along with other athletic administrators, Calvin's representatives played a major role in establishing the foundation for competition that the current MIAA membership enjoys. These men and women of the last 50 years made a significant contribution to the lives of the many students they coached, and they earned the respect and admiration of the coaches in the league. To them, sports was a medium for educating young men and women.

Rolla Anderson
Director of Athletics

I remember Kalamazoo College women athletes saying of their Calvin counterparts, "But they're so much taller and bigger than us." Yes, Calvin women's athletic teams were always a challenge for us, especially in field hockey and basketball. On the other hand, Kalamazoo women always looked forward to tennis and archery with Calvin. After all, in tennis there was a net between us, and in archery, we were not shooting at one another. Just kidding!

During my years at Kalamazoo, Calvin teams were always well coached, skillful, and a credit to their school. I admired Doris Zuidema for her coaching skills and appreciated her friendship. She served Calvin College well. I wish Calvin continued success on the athletic fields.

Tish Loveless
Women's Athletic Director and Coach

From Olivet College

[When I assumed my position at Olivet College and asked for advice from various MIAA schools], the letters I received from Calvin College made me feel like their people wanted to help us in getting Olivet started in the MIAA again.

Over the next three years I had great relationships with the Calvin coaches and administrators. We lost to them quite often, but never did they convey an air of superiority. For them, athletics was never a "win or else" situation.

Even though I eventually moved to Kalamazoo College and left coaching, I continued to respect Calvin's coaches for their fairness in all MIAA transactions. I still have lasting friendships with several of them.

"Swede" Thomas
Coach and Administrator

Because I had played at Kalamazoo, my competitive feelings regarding Calvin College started early. Barney Steen was coach back then, and I played against Tony Diekema, Don Vroon, Tom Newhof, and many others. When I came to Olivet, I coached against both Steen and Vroon. And then Tony Diekema became Calvin College's president. More recently, Jim Timmer, Sr. and Jim Timmer, Jr. have become friends of mine on the golf coaching trail.

Ralph Honderd and I coached some memorable games against each other, especially during the three years in which Olivet won the MIAA championship. [The second year of our run] we defeated Calvin by a huge score at Olivet. Ralph Honderd, who was also very competitive, congratulated me and said, "We will see you at Calvin." We did manage to defeat Calvin that time, too, but only by virtue of a last-second shot. The following year we tied with Calvin for the MIAA championship. Why were those games so special? Because it was unheard of for Olivet to defeat Calvin. We were David, and Calvin was the giant.

I have had good relationships with coaches in the MIAA, but no better than those with Barney Steen and both Jim Timmers. I also appreciate very much the support that Dave Tuuk, as athletic director, gave me at a decisive time in my career.

Gary Morrison
Basketball and Golf Coach

FACULTY ATHLETICS REPRESENTATIVES AND THE MIAA

Each college in the conference designates one faculty athletics representative to serve as a voting member on the MIAA Governing Board. The board's decisions are then sent to the Presidents' Council for adoption.

Over the past dozen years the Governing Board has gradually assumed greater involvement in the league's policy decisions and operations. Before the early 1990s, the board met twice yearly without being given prior notice as to the substance of items to appear on its agenda. Due to this practice, erratic attendance at these semi-annual meetings, and other tendencies, the board appeared to lose some of its significance as a decision-making body.

Since the early 1990s, however, the situation has changed. A committee including members of the Governing Board was appointed to review and rewrite the entire MIAA operations manual. Its decisions, which strengthened the role of faculty athletics representatives, were in turn adopted by the Presidents' Council.

At the encouragement of the league commissioner, the Governing Board also has become involved in the NCAA's Faculty Athletics Representative Association. Calvin's representative in the early 1990s, Beverly Klooster, was the first MIAA faculty athletics representative to be sent to the meetings of that association. She also served on the Interpretations and Legislative Committee of the NCAA, the body assigned the task of rewriting the entire Division III Manual. Thus the role of faculty athletics representatives has increased in significance on the national level as well as within the league itself.

A GALLERY OF CALVIN COLLEGE COACHES

Included on these pages are only varsity coaches who coached two years or longer; assistant coaches, though of great value to the various programs, are not included due to space limitations.

The designation "W" refers to women's athletics, "M" to men's.

Gregg Afman
W-Basketball, W-Track and Field

Dan Baas
M-Swimming

Deb Bakker
W-Soccer, W-Softball

Jerry Bergsma
W-Golf

Winifred Byker
W-Basketball, W-Tennis, W-Archery

James Czanko
M-Baseball

Brian Diemer
M-Cross Country

Ed Douma
M-Basketball

Esther Driesenga
W-Basketball, W-Cross Country,
W-Track and Field

Dean Ellens
W-Tennis, M-Tennis

Kim Gall
W-Basketball, W-Tennis

Dan Gelderloos
W-Swimming, M-Swimming

Lori Hageman
W-Field Hockey, W-Softball

Al Hoekstra
M-Cross Country

Ralph Honderd
M-Basketball, M-Track and Field,
W-Track and Field, W-Golf

Chris Hughes
M-Soccer

Jong-Il Kim
M-Track and Field, W-Track and Field

Ken Mange
M-Swimming, W-Swimming

Annelies Knoppers
W-Field Hockey, W-Tennis, W-Volleyball

Nancy Meyer
W-Cross Country, W-Swimming,
M-Swimming, W-Tennis

Al Lewen
M-Tennis

Albert Muyskens
M-Tennis

Mary Jo Louters
W-Track and Field

Milan Norgauer
M-Tennis

Phil Lucasse
M-Swimming

Nell Oosthoek
W-Basketball, W-Tennis

Mike Petrusma
W-Soccer

Jeff Pettinga
M-Baseball, M-Wrestling

Mark Recker
W-Soccer

Howard Rienstra
M-Tennis

Ellen Rottman
W-Basketball, W-Tennis

Mary Schutten
W-Volleyball, W-Swimming

Neil Starks
M-Wrestling

Barney Steen
M-Basketball, M-Baseball,
M-Swimming, M-Golf

Janna TerMolen
W-Softball, W-Volleyball

James Timmer, Sr.
M-Golf, M-Swimming

Karen Timmer
W-Volleyball, W-Tennis

Dave Tuuk
M-Cross Country, M-Track and Field

Kevin Vande Streek
M-Basketball

John Vanden Berg
M-Golf

Nita Vander Berg
W-Softball, W-Field Hockey

Nancy Van Noord
W-Tennis, W-Volleyball

Dave Ver Merris
M-Soccer

Don Vroon
M-Basketball, W-Basketball,
M-Baseball, M-Tennis

Amber Warners
W-Softball, W-Volleyball

James Webster
M-Wrestling

Karla Wolters
W-Baskeball, W-Softball,
W-Tennis, W-Volleyball

Doris Zuidema
W-Archery, W-Field Hockey,
W-Basketball, W-Tennis, W-Golf

Marvin Zuidema
M-Baseball, M-Soccer, M-Tennis

A. Donald Vroon
In Memoriam

We remember and recognize Coach A. Donald
Vroon (1933-2004) for his achievements as
a fine Calvin athlete in cross country, basketball, and baseball. We thank God for Coach
Vroon's 38 years as professor of physical
education, for his masterful teaching in the
basic physical education program, and for the
commitment and skill with which he coached
baseball, men's and women's basketball, and
tennis. Though we mourn his passing, we
gratefully celebrate his faithful, dedicated
service to Calvin College.

FROM THE PAST
The Development of Calvin's Athletic Facilities

With the purchase of Knollcrest Farm in 1956, Calvin's teams finally could look forward to having their own home facilities. The development of those facilities took place over a period of years.

In 1957 a cross country course, four miles in length, with no repetition loops, was developed on the new Knollcrest acreage.

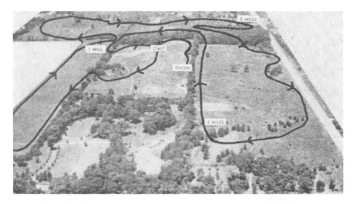

In 1960 six new tennis courts were built adjacent to Noordewier Hall.

Also in 1960, Calvin constructed an eight-lane running track with field event areas north of the tennis courts. Initial plans for a cinder surface were revised when Barney Steen heard about the University of Kentucky's asphalt-base track, which had an all-weather, rubber surface. After visiting the facility in Kentucky, Calvin vice president Henry DeWit and Steen decided to construct a similar track at Knollcrest.

Mike Vanden Bosch, a recent Calvin graduate, was commissioned to collect rubber buffings from local tire retreading companies. These materials were then processed by Michigan Colprovia Company, and the track was laid, rubber over asphalt. This revolutionary new surface was the first of its kind in the nation's far north.

In 1960 a badly needed home baseball field was begun, the rough grading done by a local contractor. A stone dust infield was laid, and the outfield was seeded.

Checking out the new track: Barry Koops, Barney Steen, Vice President Henry DeWit

In 1964, after months of careful thought, the main plans were set for the construction of the new Physical Education Building. Excitement increased as the building began to take shape. This facility was designed to fulfill a number of functions. It included five teaching stations for physical education classes, four basketball courts for practice and intramurals, and a wonderful arena which was to seat 4,500 spectators for home basketball games. The building was also eventually to accommodate visits from high-profile political candidates, professional tennis and basketball exhibitions, an occasional circus in the summer(!), state high school athletic tournaments, concerts, and more importantly, Calvin's

In the 1970s, after softball was introduced into the women's athletic program, the existing baseball field was converted into a home softball facility. Baseball was moved to a beautiful valley on the northwest corner of the campus, an area that had once been part of a nine-hole golf course called Ravenswood Country Club. After further development, this field today is probably the finest baseball facility for an NCAA Division III college in the entire Midwest.

In the late 1980s a new track surface was laid.

In the 1990s the main soccer field was provided with a new, up-to-date surface and special installations for drainage.

In 2000 the track and field facility was given a complete overhaul, the result being one of the finest facilities on any small-college campus in the Midwest.

In 2003 a new women's softball field was built across the East Beltline, east of the Prince Conference Center.

The beneficiaries of these developments have been, first of all, an entire generation—and more—of Calvin student athletes.

annual graduation exercises. The fact that the structure continues to look like new is a tribute both to its planners and architects and to the excellent preventive maintenance done by those entrusted with its upkeep.

The dedication of the building included a delightful special exhibition by a Danish gymnastics troop. An open house was held for the campus community and for Grand Rapids residents; a basketball game with Northern Michigan University completed the dedication festivities.

The beautiful prayer spoken at the dedication of this fine structure is found on the first page of Part I of this volume.

In 1974, after a number of fund-raising activities—including concession sales and Mrs. Steen's selling dill pickles at home basketball games—brought in a $50,000 check and the Bergsma family had given a generous gift toward the construction of a swimming facility, Mr. Syd Youngsma raised the remaining funds necessary for building the Bergsma Memorial Natatorium, a fine addition to the main physical education building. Physical education classes, intramurals, and intercollegiate swim meets are regularly held in the natatorium.

The Varsity Club was organized in 1949, with interest growing each year throughout most of the 1960s. Led by Bill Kooistra, a member of Calvin's golf and tennis teams, the club started on a "wild ride" all its own in 1953. Bill, one of its most aggressive and creative members, came by his interest in athletics naturally, since his father, Heinie Kooistra, had been a live wire back in the 1920s, making athletes a force on campus by doing special projects that benefited Calvin students.

As a student, Bill also had a part-time job reporting on

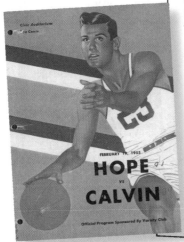

This publication is the official basketball program of Calvin College and is sponsored by the Varsity Club.

Editor-in-chief — Bill Kooistra
Assistant Editors — Rog Boer, Rog Boerema

CLUB OFFICERS

Jack Smant, President John Hoogland, Sec.
Rog Nykamp, Vice Pres. Ron Van Putten, Treas.

CLUB MEMBERS

Jim Beezhold	Fred Hoff
Rog Boer	Herm Jongsma
Rog Boerema	Lee Kikkert
Ben Boersma	Jim Kok
Bruce Bouman	Bill Kooistra
Ben Bouwman	Bob Kooistra
Don Bratt	Al Koops
Ren Broekhuizen	Tom O'Hara
Al Cok	Ed Roels
Gord De Kruyter	Arnie Rottman
Norm De Nooyer	Pete Steen
Tony Diekema	Dave Tjapkes
Pete Duyst	Mike Van Den Bosch
Mart Essenburg	Gib Vander Aa
Bernie Greenfield	Duane Vander Brug
Wayne Gritter	Pete Van Vliet
Rog Hamstra	Don Vroon
Stan Holthouse	Chuck Witteveen

Calvin sports for the *Grand Rapids Herald*, at that time the local morning paper. On occasion he would "scoop" the *Grand Rapids Press* by listing his choice of All-MIAA teams before the *Press* went to print. His accuracy was usually around 95 percent.

One of Bill's projects was to get the Coca-Cola Company to furnish the paper for basketball programs, which the Varsity

Club then sold at home games. The Club used the proceeds of this venture for many worthy causes. Special items they purchased included a brass bulletin board for the lobby of the Franklin Street Administration Building, a video camera for the school's use, a set of bleachers for overflow seating at basketball games, and a whirlpool for the health center, to be used to treat student and athlete injuries. In addition, the Club organized tennis tournaments and track meets for the Christian junior high schools and purchased sports equipment for needy schools in far away places like Nigeria, Japan, and Rehoboth Christian School in New Mexico.

Closer to home, the Club sponsored

Don Coray, Chimes sports editor, student manager in basketball, and "artist in residence," who drew the cartoons

special nights on campus, at which freshmen were invited to an evening describing the Calvin athletic program. It also sent out letters to Christian high schools, describing what Calvin had to offer.

One year the Club voted to purchase a bus from Army Surplus to be used to transport athletic teams. Naturally, it was painted yellow—gold, if you wish. It also sponsored the annual Alumni-Varsity Basketball Night, which became the traditional way to begin the basketball season. Joined to this event, at least for a time, was "Counter Courtin'" week.

One might wonder where the funds for all these projects and events came from. One prominent source, in addition to the sale of basketball programs, was a program called "Varsity Varieties," an annual show that delighted the student body with special features like its own version of "HMS Pinafore," as well as other acts performed by talented Club members.

Late in the 1960s and early 1970s, as Calvin moved to its new campus at Knollcrest, some of the camaraderie the Club previously generated began to wane, and interest waned as the student culture changed.

Nevertheless, we ought not forget all that the Varsity Club contributed in its day to the Calvin community. For many years, this club was the most active organization on campus.

A SALUTE TO ALL *CHIMES* SPORTS EDITORS AND CALVIN SPORTS INFORMATION DIRECTORS

Before 1981, when Fred De Haan was hired, Calvin did not have a sports information director. The college had to rely on the sports editor of *Chimes* to cover what had happened with the various teams during the week past. Those early *Chimes* sports editors deserve a special salute for their good work during the years prior to 1981.

In 1985 Phil de Haan was appointed to the SID position. When he was promoted to director of media relations in 1993, Jeff Febus replaced him as sports information director. For 10 years now, Febus has done an excellent job, instituting, among other things, the Calvin Sports Hot Line (616-526-6522), which comes on nightly and summarizes the day's activities.

The coming of web communications, with the demand for instant and complete scores and information, has added significant challenge to the SID position. Even with talented student assistance, it is only the "above the call of duty" effort of Febus that keeps the Calvin faithful (for the most part) happy.

Of course, part of the reason for a busy SID is successful teams, coaches, and athletes—and Calvin has been blessed with many!

CALVIN COLLEGE AS HOST OF NCAA DIVISION III CHAMPIONSHIP EVENTS

During approximately the last quarter-century Calvin has hosted ten NCAA national championship events in three different sports. Doing so has been both a privilege and a challenge.

In 1977 and 1978 the NCAA Division III men's track and field championships were held at Calvin. Preparing for them required the exercise of extraordinary organizational skills at a variety of levels, from the college's food service to its housing office to its campus security department. Needless to say, however, the bulk of the work fell on the staff of the Physical Education Department, whose task was complicated by the amount of detail involved in hosting such an event.

Calvin's facilities were in top shape and were fully adequate to meet the needs of the teams that came from all over the United States. Since the meets were held after the conclusion of the academic year, most of the competing athletes stayed in the dormitories and ate in the dining hall. The close proximity of both facilities proved to be advantageous for practice purposes.

The wider Calvin community, including faculty members and alumni, helped with timing and judging the various contests. The greater Grand Rapids community also lent its support in many ways and turned out in goodly number to witness these prestigious events. One of the highlights of the 1977 championships was the entry in the 400-meter intermediate hurdles of Edwin Moses, the gold medal winner in the 1976 Olympics. Another was a breakfast of the Fellowship of Christian Athletes featuring an address by Jim Ryan, the country's premier 1500-meter runner.

Hosting these two events helped give Calvin national recognition. An abundance of grateful, appreciative comments by many of the hundreds of athletes who participated in these championships were in themselves an adequate reward for the considerable work involved in putting them on.

The Physical Education Department staff's successful experience with the track and field championships in 1977 and 1978 gave it confidence that it could perform a similar service in basketball. As a result, Calvin applied to be the host for the basketball finals in 1982. NCAA officials, no doubt somewhat influenced by the college's performance with track and field in 1977 and 1978, accepted Calvin's invitation.

Since school was in full session during the basketball championships, logistics became somewhat more complicated. Teams could no longer stay in student resident halls, but were housed in the Harley Hotel on the corner of East Paris Avenue and Cascade Road. Coach Don Vroon took on the formidable task of seeing that the sometimes complex needs of the various teams from all corners of the nation were met, and did so with consummate skill and success. Once again, Calvin proved to be up to the challenge it had taken on.

The P.E. Department adjusted its schedule of activities so that practice times could be arranged for all participating squads. On Thursday evening a banquet was held at the Grand Plaza Hotel in downtown Grand Rapids for the teams and NCAA officials. Semi-final games were played Friday evening, and the finals were held on Saturday.

Because the tournament had gone so smoothly, the NCAA committee asked if it could be held at Calvin the next year, 1983, as well. What eventually developed was a series of seven consecutive championships hosted by Calvin. Unfortunately, no Calvin team qualified for the tournament during these years; as a result, the games were not sell-outs. Community support of the project was nevertheless solid.

Calvin's next venture in hosting an NCAA Division III championship event took place in 1986 and involved women's volleyball. As the historical sketch found in Part I of this book indicates, Calvin fielded an especially strong team that year, qualified for the Final Four, and was asked to serve as host school for the tournament semi-finals and finals. Women's ath-letic director Doris Zuidema and volleyball coach Karla Wolt-ers did a fine job of organizing this complex event, despite the time constraints within which they had to operate.

Calvin won the semi-final game but lost in the finals to the University of California–San Diego before an enthusiastic crowd of 3,500 fans. Despite that loss, the entire experience of hosting and playing in the tournament was eminently worthwhile.

RADIO VOICES OF CALVIN BASKETBALL

S oon after Calvin's entry into the MIAA, local sportscast-ers began broadcasting men's basketball games, both home and away. For nearly a half-century they have performed notable service and deserve recognition for their contributions to the program.

Al Ackerman broadcast Calvin games on WOOD radio from 1954-1961.

Warren Reynolds succeeded Ackerman, broadcasting on WOOD radio from 1962-1970; he also did the commentary for Hope-Calvin TV games from 1966-1996.

Tom Brown and others filled the gap between Warren Reynolds and Doug Wentworth.

Doug Wentworth broadcast Calvin games on WJBL radio (Holland) from 1962-1983, and since 1984 has been heard on WFUR, where he continues his excellent work. In recent years, Wentworth has extended WFUR coverage to a number of women's basketball games as well.

Warren Reynolds   *Doug Wentworth*

CHEERLEADERS

In the early decades of Calvin basketball, cheerleaders were called "yell masters." These yell masters originally were uninhibited students who readily moved onto the floor to lead cheers. Student fans responded enthusiastically to them and to their eventual successors, organized cheerleading squads composed of both men and women, until well after World War II.

In the late 1960s and early 1970s, however, attitudes began to change. Not only did students become lethargic about organized cheering, but in some cases they even came close to mocking their own cheerleaders. This development eventually led to the quiet demise of organized cheerleading squads.

As the years passed, the student section at basketball games became a body that spontaneously erupted with their own cheers. Furthermore, the pep band seems to have taken up and directed some of the enthusiasm formerly generated by cheerleaders. On occasion, visiting teams do bring along their version of those earlier cheerleaders, but these groups do not lead cheers; they perform gymnastic feats—and sometimes are aped by our exuberant student fans.

When games get particularly tense, Chaplain Cooper, who grew up in a different day, has been known to charge out onto the floor to lead cheers. Even without his help, however, the gold-shirted student section still can "raise the roof" in hotly contested basketball games. Keep it up!

SPECIAL CONTRIBUTIONS TO CALVIN'S PROGRAM

Unsung Heroes—But "All-Stars"

Lena Leegwater worked hard for many years, washing, mending, and ironing to make sure students had clean uniforms for P.E. classes and athletic contests.

Barbara Keefer was department secretary extraordinaire. For 33 years she took care of staff needs for all facets of the physical education and athletics programs and saw to the details of countless special events.

For 15 years Jack Betten was custodian in the new Physical Education Building, keeping the structure looking like new and preparing the home facilities, both inside and out of doors, for athletic contests. Jack could fix anything that needed repair, and even built a pitching machine for the baseball team in his spare time.

Charlie Huizenga, grounds superintendent, has worked tirelessly for many years, making Calvin's outdoor athletic facilities look first-class.

Dick Wilkins has held the position of equipment manager for the past 25 years, setting up for home athletic contests and keeping inventory of equipment for all sports, intramural programs, and physical education classes.

To all of these special people: many thanks for serving so faithfully!

Lena Leegwater

Charlie Huizenga

Barb Keefer

Jack Betten

Dick Wilkins

Two Standouts in Men's Basketball

Mark Veenstra

Steve Honderd

Calvin's rich tradition in men's basketball has seen the emergence and development of literally hundreds of excellent players. However, two athletes in that select group stand out by virtue of their extraordinary contributions to Calvin's program.

MARK VEENSTRA, 1973-1977

Among Mark's achievements are the following:
– Voted an All-MIAA player for four years
– Named conference MVP four times
– Earned All-American recognition
– Designated an NCAA post-graduate scholar

Because of MIAA Governing Board policy then in force, the fine teams on which Mark played were not allowed to participate in post-season play. That policy obviously is no longer in effect.

STEVE HONDERD, 1989-1993

Among Steve's achievements are the following:
– Voted an All-MIAA player for four years
– Named conference MVP twice
– Earned All-American honors
– Designated an NCAA post-graduate scholar

In addition to receiving these honors, Steve was given the exceptional distinction of being named NCAA Division III Player of the Decade.

Five Softball Pitchers
Who Made a Difference

A softball team's success or failure depends to an unusual degree on the quality of its pitching. The five exceptional pitchers featured below deserve special recognition for their contributions to Calvin's program. During their careers they set MIAA records that still stand today, were voted league MVPs, and were instrumental in their team's championship performances.

Jessica Schrier
1984-1987

Shauna Koolhaas
1995-1998

Sharon Boeve
1982-1985

Laura Vroon
1981-1984

Kristi Klaasen
1988-1991

Three Generations of Broenes

The Broene tradition in Calvin basketball began before World War II, when Gene, a former high school star from Grand Rapids Christian, played for Coach Muyskens' Knights for one season before entering the service. In 1945-46 he returned to Calvin, this time joining Coach Chuck Bult's squad and setting a single-game scoring record of 39 points.

Two of Gene and Jeanne's children attended Calvin in the 1970s. Greg was a talented member of the basketball team and an accomplished tennis player. Like Greg, his sister Debbie also starred in both sports, excelling in women's basketball and playing the number one position on the women's tennis team.

From 2002 through 2004 Greg and Betsy's son, Kevin, represented the third Broene generation, playing three years of solid basketball on the men's team. The Calvin community gratefully notes the combination of loyalty and skill shown by this remarkable family.

Broene Family: Greg, Gene, Jeanne, Kevin
Inset: Debbie Broene

A GLIMPSE INTO THE CALVIN-HOPE RIVALRY IN MEN'S BASKETBALL

Calvin notches 22nd straight win over Hope

By Leo Martonosi
Sentinel sports editor

GRAND RAPIDS — The beat goes. And it's not the type of music that turns on Hope College basketball coach Glenn Van Wieren.

The Calvin College Knights continued their winning ways in the MIAA opener against their rivals from Holland by trimming the Flying Dutchmen Saturday in Knollcrest Fieldhouse before a packed house, 66-54.

Calvin has now taken the last 22 games between the two teams. Hope hasn't beaten the Knights since the final game of the 1967-68 season.

"Getting a win here today was more important than the finesse of the game because of our last three games," stated Calvin coach Don Vroon. "After losing our last three games (all on the road) we had a bit of a confidence problem.

"We played our best basketball during the first 10 minutes of the first half," added Vroon. "We should have busted the game open the next 10 minutes, but you have to give Hope credit for hanging in there.

"The sun will shine tomorrow," said Van Wieren. "We'll practice Monday and we'll play Wednesday.

"We got 11 league games left and we'll be back and we'll play better," he insisted.

Both teams performed like they would have had a tough time beating a good high school club.

The Knights did have the muscle underneath in 6-foot 8-inch Marty Grasmeyer. That's one of the reasons they won the league opener and are 6-4 for the season.

Grasmeyer cleared 18 rebounds which was almost as high as Hope's 25 team effort. The Knights plucked 41 missed shots off both ends of the court.

Hope never led in the game as Calvin grabbed a 20-10 lead and coasted the rest of the way home.

The Dutchmen did cut the gap to two points in the beginning — 22-20 — on some heads up play by subsitute guard Rick Reece.

However, turnovers and the inability to find the hoop resulted in Calvin notching 10 unanswered points.

Tom VanderStel's basket at the buzzer cut Calvin's halftime advantage to 10 points at 32-22.

A dunk by Grasmeyer bought out many yellow handkerchiefs that the Calvin students were waving throughout the contest. His slam gave the Knights a commanding 20-point, 47-27 margin.

Bruce Capel, who preped at Hudsonville Unity, sank a free throw to up Calvin's lead to 21 points moments later.

A few bad passes by the Knights made the final score much closer statistically than it actually was graphically.

Grasmeyer was the game's high point man with 15 markers. Johnny King added 14 counters, Don Danhoff, 11 and Stacy, 10. Scott Benson was Hope's top gunner with 14 points. Dale Wolfe came off the bench to throw in 10.

Hope pumped in one more fielder than Calvin, 22-21 but couldn't find the lid from the free throw lane. The Dutchmen were only able to hit on 10 of 24 freebies for a frigid 41 percent clip.

Calvin was 24 of 34 from the line for 70 percent and 21 of 52 from the floor...

As the listing of game results printed on the following pages shows, during the decade from 1969 to 1979 Calvin won 22 games in a row against our neighbor to the west, Hope College. Coach Vroon's team began this run by winning twice, Coach Honderd's teams continued it by winning the next 15 games, and after Vroon resumed coaching duties in 1977, his teams won the next five. Not until the second semester of the 1979-80 season was Hope able to stop this streak. It seems highly unlikely that anything like this will ever happen again. *(Please see article from the* Holland Sentinel *of January 14, 1980.)* Hope's longest win streak occurred between 1994 and 1998, when the Dutch won 10 consecutive games against Calvin.

Since entering the MIAA in the 1953-54 season, the Knights hold a 64-49 series advantage over Hope. During that 50-year period, Calvin has outscored Hope by 368 points, for an average of 3.3 points per game. Most of the games have been very close; 11 of them went into overtime. Calvin has won seven of the last 10 meetings, but Hope has won three of the last four. During the past 50 years, Calvin won or shared the MIAA title 26 times, while Hope has taken or shared the title 21 times. Only three times was neither Hope nor Calvin champion or co-champion.

Calvin-Hope Game Results – 1953-2003

Season	Coach	Winner
1950s		
1953-1954	Steen	Calvin
	Steen	Hope
1954-1955	Steen	Calvin
	Steen	Hope
1955-1956	Steen	Calvin
	Steen	Hope
1956-1957	Steen	Calvin
	Steen	Hope
1957-1958	Steen	Hope
	Steen	Hope
1958-1959	Steen	Calvin
	Steen	Hope
1960s		
1959-1960	Steen	Hope
	Steen	Hope
1960-1961	Steen	Calvin
	Steen	Calvin
1961-1962	Steen	Calvin
	Steen	Hope
1962-1963	Steen	Hope
	Steen	Hope
1963-1964	Steen	Calvin
	Steen	Calvin
1964-1965	Steen	Calvin
	Steen	Hope
1965-1966	Steen	Hope
	Steen	Calvin
1966-1967	Vroon	Hope
	Vroon	Hope
1967-1968	Vroon	Hope
	Vroon	Calvin
1968-1969	Vroon	Calvin
	Vroon	Hope
1970s		
1969-1970	Vroon	Calvin
	Vroon	Calvin
1970-1971	Honderd	Calvin
	Honderd	Calvin
1971-1972	Honderd	Calvin
	Honderd	Calvin
1972-1973	Honderd	Calvin
	Honderd	Calvin
1973-1974	Honderd	Calvin
	Honderd	Calvin
1974-1975	Honderd	Calvin
	Honderd	Calvin
1975-1976	Honderd	Calvin
	Honderd	Calvin
1976-1977	Honderd	Calvin
	Honderd	Calvin
1977-1978	Vroon	Calvin
	Vroon	Calvin
1978-1979	Vroon	Calvin
	Vroon	Calvin
1980s		
1979-1980	Vroon	Calvin
	Vroon	Hope
1980-1981	Vroon	Calvin
	Vroon	Hope
1981-1982	Vroon	Calvin
	Vroon	Hope
1982-1983	Vroon	Hope
	Vroon	Hope
1983-1984	Vroon	Hope
	Vroon	Hope
1984-1985	Douma	Hope
	Douma	Hope
1985-1986	Douma	Calvin
	Douma	Hope
1986-1987	Douma	Hope
	Douma	Hope
	Douma	Calvin
1987-1988	Douma	Hope
	Douma	Calvin
1988-1989	Douma	Calvin
	Douma	Calvin
1990s		
1989-1990	Douma	Calvin
	Douma	Calvin
	Douma	Calvin
1990-1991	Douma	Hope
	Douma	Hope
	Douma	Calvin
1991-1992	Douma	Calvin
	Douma	Calvin
1992-1993	Douma	Calvin
	Douma	Calvin
	Douma	Calvin
1993-1994	Douma	Calvin
	Douma	Calvin
1994-1995	Douma	Hope
	Douma	Hope
1995-1996	Douma	Hope
	Douma	Hope
1996-1997	Vande Streek	Hope
	Vande Streek	Hope
	Vande Streek	Hope
1997-1998	Vande Streek	Hope
	Vande Streek	Hope
1998-1999	Vande Streek	Calvin
	Vande Streek	Hope
2000-2003		
1999-2000	Vande Streek	Calvin
	Vande Streek	Calvin
2000-2001	Vande Streek	Calvin
	Vande Streek	Calvin
2001-2002	Vande Streek	Calvin
	Vande Streek	Hope
2002-2003	Vande Streek	Calvin
	Vande Streek	Hope
	Vande Streek	Hope

SINGLE GAME, INDIVIDUAL SCORING RECORDS IN BASKETBALL

Women's Basketball

Points	Player	Opponent	Date
40	Eileen Boonstra	Kalamazoo	2-23-80
36	Cara Mulder	Oakland	11-25-94
35	Pam Wubben	Alma	2-19-94
32	Kathy DeBoer	Michigan State	2-28-75
32	Yvonne VanGoor	Michigan State	2-16-67
31	Karen Langeland	Goshen	2-3-67
30	Leanne Bajema	St. Mary's	2-26-92
30	Deb Broene	Lake Superior	3-1-79
30	Deb Broene	Grand Valley	1-25-79
29	Robyn Fennema	Saginaw Valley	11-26-99
29	Kim Bartman	Adrian	2-19-92
29	Julie Post	Adrian	1-24-87
29	Deb Broene	U. of Michigan	2-3-79
29	Deb Broene	Hope	1-20-79
29	Kathy DeBoer	UW-Oshkosh	3-2-75
28	Pam Wubben	Adrian	2-13-93
28	Beth Hollander	Albion	2-25-93
28	Beth Hollander	Grand Valley	12-1-92
28	Sue Vander Molen	Olivet	2-9-85
28	Diane Spoelstra	Central Michigan	1-31-74
28	Karen Langeland	Michigan State	3-4-69
28	Lena Baker	Michigan State	2-16-67
28	Yvonne Van Goor	GRJC	1-26-67
28	Eleanor Danhof	Hope	1963

Men's Basketball

Points	Player	Opponent	Date
61	Steve Honderd	Kalamazoo	2-20-93
56	Mark Veenstra	Adrian	1-31-76
53	Mike Phelps	Concordia, IL	1-27-68
52	Mark Veenstra	Biola, CA	1-3-76
52	Duane Rosendahl	Olivet	2-20-52
41	Todd Hennink	Malone, OH	11-24-90
40	Chris Knoester	La Verne, CA	12-31-93
40	Mark Veenstra	Alma	2-29-76
39	Pres Kool	Alma	2-13-53
38	Scott Plaisier	Illinois Benedictine	11-21-98
38	Steve Honderd	Alma	2-28-92
38	Steve Honderd	Alma	2-2-91
38	Dan Davis	GR Baptist	12-8-88
38	Dan Davis	Olivet	2-17-88
38	Bill Sall	Hope	3-7-87
38	Mark Veenstra	S. Colorado State	1-2-76
38	Duane Rosendahl	Kalamazoo	12-6-50
37	Mark Veenstra	Alma	1-9-75
36	Ryan Stahr	Alma	1-26-95
36	Steve Honderd	North Park, IL	12-29-90
36	Dan Davis	Hope	2-8-89
36	Dan Davis	Ferris State	12-7-88

NATIONAL ACADEMIC AWARDS WON BY CALVIN ATHLETES

NCAA Post Graduate Scholarships

John Brink '83	Cross country and track; engineering major.
Steve Honderd '93	Basketball; economics major.
Joel Klooster '02	Cross country; electrical engineering major.
Amy Kuipers '96	Cross country and track; nursing major.
Ray VanArragon '95	Cross country and track; philosophy and religion major.
Peter Vande Brake '87	Track and field; philosophy major.
Mark Veenstra '77	Basketball and track; biology and physical education major.

CoSIDA (College Sports Information Directors' Association) Academic All-Americans

Basketball

1992	Steve Honderd
1993	Steve Honderd
1993	Chris Knoester
1994	Chris Knoester*
1999	Aaron Winkle
2000	Aaron Winkle

Cross Country/Track and Field

1994	Ray Van Arragon
1995	Ray Van Arragon
1996	Holly Breuker, Betsy Haverkamp, Amy Kuipers
1997	Andrea Clark, Betsy Haverkamp
1998	Andrea Clark
1999	Andrea Clark, Sarah Gritter, Cara Jansen, Steve Michmerhuizen, Phil Sikkenga, Scott Westhouse
2000	Sarah Gritter, Joel Klooster
2001	Erinn Boot, Mark DeWeerd, Sarah Gritter, Joel Klooster, Paul Petersen, Phil Sikkenga
2002	Erinn Boot, Dan Hoekstra, Joel Klooster,** David Ritsema
2003	Joel Klooster

*Named Academic All-American of the Year in men's basketball

**Named Academic All-American of the Year in men's cross country/track and field

Soccer

1996	Sam Glass, William Watts
1997	Sam Glass, Cara Jansen
1998	Cara Jansen
2003	Joel Veldhouse

Softball

1983	Sharon Boeve
1989	Laurie Hiemstra
1997	Melanie Bolt, Melanie Harriff, Shauna Koolhaas
1998	Melanie Harriff, Shauna Koolhaas

Volleyball

1986	Julie Dykstra

ATHLETIC AND LEADERSHIP AWARDS GRANTED BY CALVIN COLLEGE

Joe Beré

The Beré Memorial Award

The Harold "Joe" Beré Award was inaugurated in 1951 by the Varsity Club, with the approval of the Beré family. Joe Beré, a Calvin pre-law student, was an avid sports fan who was fatally injured while en route to a Calvin basketball game against Ferris in Big Rapids. This prestigious award is granted each year to a senior male athlete, and is based on the recipient's leadership and achievements in athletics and academic work, as well as on his character and his contributions to his team(s) while at Calvin.

1951	Sam Cooper	Basketball and track and field
1952	Duane Rosendahl	Basketball and tennis
1953	Roger Postmus	Basketball and tennis
1955	Morris Tubergen	Cross country and track and field
1956	A. Donald Vroon	Cross country, basketball, and baseball
1957	Norm DeNooyer	Baseball
1958	Tom Newhof	Basketball
1960	Ken Tanis	Cross country and track and field
1961	Barry Koops	Cross country and track and field
1962	Carl DeKuiper	Basketball and baseball
1963	Casey TerHaar	Soccer
1964	Jim Van Eerden	Basketball
1965	Ken Fletcher	Basketball and baseball
1966	Jerry Terpsma	Soccer
1967	Bert DeLeeuw	Tennis
1968	Dave Ver Merris	Track and field, swimming, and soccer
1969	Rudy Vlaardingerbroek	Swimming and track and field
1970	Mark VerWys	Swimming
1971	Randy Commeret	Wrestling and baseball
1972	Bob Bosch	Basketball and track and field

1973	Art Tuls	Basketball
1974	Greg Broene	Basketball and tennis
1975	Larry VanderVeen	Basketball
1976	Gregg Afman	Basketball and track and field
1977	Mark Veenstra	Basketball and track and field
1978	Dwight Maliepaard	Basketball
1979	Jon Houseward	Track and field
1980	Mark Stacy	Golf, soccer, and basketball
1981	Doug Diekema	Cross country and track and field
1982	Dirk Pruis	Swimming
1983	John Brink	Cross country and track
1984	Doug DeSmit	Soccer
1985	Dan Diekema	Cross country and track
1986	Steve Ruiter	Swimming
1987	Kevin VanDuyn	Basketball and baseball
1988	Peter VandeBrake	Track and field
1990	Jim Timmer, Jr.	Basketball and baseball
	John Lumkes	Cross country and track and field
1991	Ed Wilgenburg	Soccer
1992	Thad Karnehm	Cross country and track and field
1993	Steve Honderd	Basketball
1994	Chris Knoester	Basketball and baseball
1995	Ray VanArragon	Cross county and track and field
1996	Mike Lubbers	Swimming
1997	Jon Vander Ark	Tennis
1998	Dave Meester	Tennis
1999	Steve Michmerhuizen	Track and field
2000	Aaron Winkle	Basketball
2001	Phil Sikkenga	Track and field
2002	Dan Hoekstra	Cross country and track and field
2003	Joel Klooster	Cross country and track and field

Kay Tiemersma

The Kay Tiemersma Award

This prestigious award was established in 1975 and honors Kay Tiemersma, a pioneering figure in the women's physical education program at Calvin. It is granted each year to a senior who has distinguished herself in intercollegiate athletics and in the classroom, as well as by virtue of her character and contributions to her team(s).

Year	Name	Sport
1975	Ellen Mills	Field hockey and volleyball
1976	Mary Schutten	Field hockey and basketball
1977	Bonnie Knaack	Field hockey
1978	Diane Koning	Volleyball
1979	Nancy Martin	Field hockey and softball
1980	Julie Besteman	Field hockey and track and field
1981	Leslie Shaw	Field hockey and softball
1982	Deb Bakker	Field hockey and softball
1983	Deb Dykstra	Field hockey
1984	Laura Vroon	Cross country and softball
1985	Sharon Boeve	Basketball and softball
1986	Kim Lautenbach	Volleyball and track and field
1987	Sari Brummel	Diving
1988	Liesl Pruis	Swimming
1989	Leslie Tanis	Field hockey
1990	Amber Blankespoor	Volleyball and softball
	Stephanie Rhind	Swimming
1991	Sarah Ondersma	Basketball and softball
1992	Julie Overway	Field hockey, basketball, and softball
1993	Becky Konyndyk	Cross country and track and field
	Betsy Wilgenburg	Volleyball and track and field
1994	Karen Blankespoor	Volleyball and softball
1995	Holly Ondersma	Softball
1996	Amy Kuipers	Cross country and track and field
1997	Betsy Haverkamp	Cross country and track and field
1998	Shauna Koolhaas	Softball
1999	Kristi Van Woerkom	Swimming and track and field
2000	Sarah Gritter	Cross county and track and field
2001	Rhonda Volkers	Softball and volleyball
2002	Rachel Veltkamp	Track and field
2003	Annie Vander Laan	Track and field

NATIONAL ATHLETIC AWARDS WON BY CALVIN ATHLETES

National Champions in Individual Events

As has been noted in Part One of this volume, six Calvin teams have won NCAA Division III national championships: two have been in men's basketball, two in women's cross country, and two in men's cross country. These teams have been highlighted in the narrative account of the history of their sport at Calvin.

In addition, a number of individual Calvin athletes have been national champions in their event. This involves both talent and unusual discipline. These remarkable Calvin student-athletes deserve special recognition.

Four men on Calvin's track and field teams have been national champions:

> Pat McNamara   (steeplechase) 1989
> John Lumkes   (steeplechase)   1990
> Rick Lubbers   (pole vault)   1991
> J.D. Stien   (decathlon)   1996

One member of Calvin's women's cross country team has won that honor:

> Renea Bluekamp   1993

Bluekamp

A number of individuals and teams in women's track and field also were national champions:

> Angie Feinauer (long jump)   1993
>
> Patsy Orkar, Angie Feinauer,
> Kathy Haddox, Shawn Farmer
> (4x400 meter relay)   1993

Feinauer

McNamara   **Lumkes**   **Lubbers**   **Stien**

Farmer, Orkar, Haddox, Feinauer

Shawn Farmer, Holly Breuker,
Melissa Dykstra, Kathy Haddox
(4x400 meter relay)   1994

Breuker   Haverkamp   Pierce   Mulder

Haddox, Dykstra, Breuker, Farmer

Holly Breuker (400 meter hurdles)   1996

Betsy Haverkamp (3,000 meter run)   1997

Sara Veltkamp, Megan Pierce,
Lindsay Mulder, Kristi Van Woerkom
(4x400 meter relay)   1999

Megan Pierce (400 meter dash)   1999

Megan Pierce (400 meter dash)   2000

Lindsay Mulder, Megan Pierce,
Mindy Worst, Sara Veltkamp
(4x400 meter relay)   2000

Lindsay Mulder (long jump)   2001

Lindsay Mulder, Megan Pierce,
Mindy Worst, Sara Veltkamp
(4x400 meter relay)   2001

Annie Vander Laan (heptathlon)   2003

Front: Van Woerkom, Mulder; Back: Veltkamp, Pierce

Vander Laan

Front: Worst, Veltkamp; Back: Pierce, Mulder

National Champion Teams

Men's Varsity Basketball 1992 — *Back (l. to r.): Coach Ed Douma, Rob Orange, Mike Le Febre, Steve Honderd, Mike Langeland, B.J. Westra, Mark Lodewyk, Brad Capel, Asst. Coach Gregg Afman; Front: Matt Rottman, Ryan Stevens, Chris Knoester, Mark Hofman, Matt Harrison, Steve Scholler, Asst. Coach Jim Timmer, Sr.*

Men's Varsity Basketball 2000 — *Back (l. to r.): Asst. Coach Chris Fear, Asst. Coach Tim VanDyke, Aaron Winkle, Jeremy Veenstra, Brian Krosschell, Derek Kleinheksel, Josh Tubergen, Jon Vander Plas, Coach Kevin Vande Streek; Front: Jon Potvin, Nate Burgess, Dave Bartels, Nate Karsten, Nick Ploegstra, Tim Bruinsma, Jason DeKuiper, Kyle Smith, Bryan Foltice*

1998 Women's Cross Country — *Back (l. to r.): Sarah Gritter, Sara Crowe, Kris Lumkes, Kristi Brown, Rashel Bayes, April De Korte, Amy Mizzone, Emily Hollender, Asst. Coach Al Hoekstra; Middle (back to front): Allison Cook, Andrea Clark, Lindsay Carrier; Front: Student Coach Rachel Schoenfuhs, Coach Nancy Meyer, Erinn Boot, Kate Vander Schaaf, Liz Kuipers, Lisa Timmer, Sarah Gibson, Kristie De Young, Beth Giessel, Candice Vandergriff*

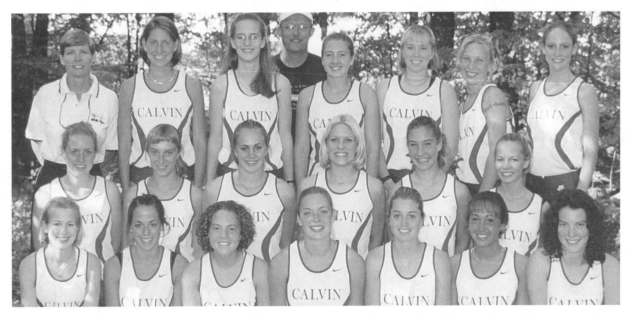

1999 Women's Cross Country — *Back (l. to r.): Coach Nancy Meyer, Kris Lumkes, Sarah Gritter, Asst. Coach Al Hoekstra, Becky Horton, Laura Medema, Holly Petkewicz, Heather Van Vugt; Middle: Emily Hollender, Katie Van Beek, April De Korte, Molly Delcamp, Lindsay Carrier; Front: Erinn Boot, Amy Mizzone, Rashel Bayes, Lisa Timmer, Liz Kuipers, Sara Skodinski, Beth Giessel*

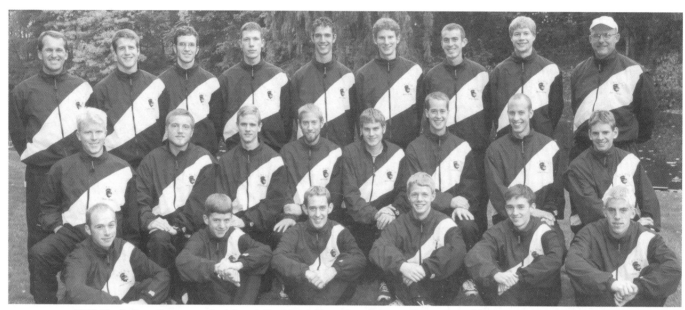

2000 Men's Cross Country — Back (l. to r.): Coach Brian Diemer, Peter Armstrong, Kevin VerBeek, Ryan Malott, Mark Lubbers, David Ritsema, Brian Paff, Justin Pfruender, Coach Al Hoekstra; Middle: Cameron Harrison, Matt Sicilia, Dan Mays, Paul Petersen, Joel Klooster, Tim VanHaitsma, Dan Hoekstra, Asst. Coach Robert Hyde; Front: Abe Huyser-Honig, Kris Koster, Tim Avery, Joel Reasoner, Matt Edwards, Kyle Carrick

2003 Men's Cross Country — Back (l. to r.): Coach Al Hoekstra, Brian Paff, Joel Alberts, David Haagsma, Todd Schuster, Jeff Engbers, Andy Yazzie; Middle: Asst. Coach Tim VanHaitsma, Kris Koster, Tim Finnegan, Ben Hammer, Hendrik Kok, Aaron Iverson, Tyler Zwagerman, Coach Brian Diemer; Front: Harrison Jorritsma, Tim Avery, Joel Reasoner, Paul Rollet, Matt Edwards, Asst. Coach Robert Hyde

CALVIN COLLEGE
ALL-AMERICANS

Baseball

1985   Kevin VanDuyn

1987   Kevin VanDuyn

Basketball - Men

1958   Tom Newhof

1977   Mark Veenstra

1989   Dan Davis, Bill Sall

1990   Bill Sall

1992   Steve Honderd

1993   Steve Honderd

2000   Aaron Winkle

2002   Jeremy Veenstra

Cross Country – Women

1992   Laura Erffmeyer, Amy Kuipers

1993   Renea Bluekamp, Betsy Haverkamp, Amy Kuipers

1994   Betsy Haverkamp, Amy Kuipers, Amy Rideout

1995   Betsy Haverkamp, Amy Kuipers

1996   Betsy Haverkamp, Lisa Timmer

1998   Andrea Clark, Amy Mizzone, Lisa Timmer

1999   Liz Kuipers, Amy Mizzone, Lisa Timmer

2001   Rachel Baber

2002   Sarah Hastings, Jessie Lair

2003   Sarah Hastings, Jessie Lair

Cross Country – Men

1960   Barry Koops, Jim DeBie

1978   Doug Diekema

1979   Doug Diekema

1980   John Brink, Kurt Mast

1981   John Brink

1982   John Brink, Kurt Mast

1987   Adam Suarez

1988   Adam Suarez

1989   Adam Suarez

1991   Rich Church

1992   Ray VanArragon

1993   Ray VanArragon

1994   Robert Hyde, Ray VanArragon

1996   Nate Lewis

1997   Kent Frens

1998   Geoff Van Dragt, Scott Westhouse

1999   Justin Pfruender

2000   Cameron Harrison, Dan Hoekstra, Joel Klooster, Justin Pfruender, Paul Peterson

2001   Dan Hoekstra, Joel Klooster, Brian Maat, Justin Pfruender

2002   Hendrik Kok, Brian Maat

2003   Tim Avery, Matt Edwards, Tim Finnegan, David Haagsma, Hendrik Kok, Kris Koster

Field Hockey - Women

1987   Leslie Tanis

1990   Kim Tanis

Soccer – Men

1962   Casey TerHaar

1983   Doug DeSmit

1991   Joey Barone

Soccer – Women

| 1997 | Tara Dyk, Amber Wiersma |
| 1998 | Tara Dyk |

Softball

1985	Sharon Boeve
1990	Kristi Klaasen
1995	Shauna Koolhaas
1996	Shauna Koolhaas
1997	Melanie Harriff, Shauna Koolhaas

Swimming - Women

1984	Sari Brummel
1985	Sari Brummel, Karen Dekker, Liesl VandeCreek
1986	Sari Brummel
1987	Sari Brummel, Stephanie Rhind, Liesl Pruis
1989	Stephanie Rhind
1994	Kathleen Shaughnessy
1999	Kaity Conrad, Erin Kloostra, Erica Smith, Kristi VanWoerkom
2000	Kaity Conrad, Erin Kloostra, Anne Kuiper, Katie Nagelkirk
2001	Kaity Conrad, Erin Kloostra, Anne Kuiper, Katie Nagelkirk

Swimming – Men

1980	Dirk Pruis
1981	Dirk Pruis
1982	Dirk Pruis
1983	Steve Ruiter
1984	Steve Ruiter
1985	Steve Ruiter, Bill VanEe
1986	Steve Ruiter
1993	Mike Lubbers
1994	Mike Lubbers
1995	Mike Lubbers
1996	Mike Lubbers
2001	Dan Hekman, A.J. Penninga, Chris Veltman, Brad White
2002	Peter Boumgarden, Dan Hekman, A.J. Penninga, Ryan Preston, Brad White
2003	Peter Boumgarden, Ryan Johnson, A.J. Penninga, Brad White

Track and Field – Men

1967	Dave VerMerris, Rudy Vlaardingerbroek
1974	Gregg Afman
1975	Gregg Afman
1976	Gregg Afman, Ben Beversluis, Joel Cooper, Jon Houseward, Ben Ridder
1977	Dave Alkema, Gary Mulder, Ben Ridder, Randy VanDyken
1978	Randy Veenstra
1985	Pete VandeBrake
1986	Pete VandeBrake
1987	Pat McNamara, Dan Owen, Pete VandeBrake, Dean VanderHill
1988	Pat McNamara, Dan Owen, Pete VandeBrake, Norm Zylstra
1989	Brian Davis, John Lumkes, Pat McNamara, Dan Owen, Robb Steenwyk
1990	Rick Lubbers, John Lumkes, Robb Steenwyk, David Sydow, Craig Tanis
1991	Thad Karnehm, Rick Lubbers, Steve Seth, David Sydow, Craig Tanis
1992	Thad Karnehm, Rick Lubbers, Steve Seth, David Sydow
1993	Matt Schellenberg, Steve Seth, Mark Ver Merris, Derk Walkotten
1994	Ray Van Arragon, Mark Ver Merris
1995	Nate Lewis, J.D. Stien, Ray Van Arragon, Jason Washler
1996	J.D. Stien
1997	Lee Doherty, Nate Lewis, J.D. Stien
1998	Steve Michmerhuizen, Geoff VanDragt
1999	Mark DeWeerd, Lee Doherty, Eric Hansen, Dan Hoekstra, Derek Kleinheksel, Jay Lumkes, Steve Michmerhuizen, Curt Mulder, Phil Sikkenga
2000	Steve Abbring, Eric Hansen, Derek Kleinheksel, Joel Klooster, Phil Sikkenga, Keith VanGoor
2001	Steve Abbring, Cameron Baron, Mark DeWeerd, Eric Hansen, Dan Hoekstra, Derek Kleinheksel, Justin Pfreunder, Phil Sikkenga, Keith VanGoor
2002	Dan Hoekstra, Joel Klooster, Hendrik Kok, Justin Pfreunder, Keith VanGoor
2003	Joel Klooster, Hendrik Kok, Nate Meckes, Andy Yazzie

Track and Field – Women

1982	Emke Vreugdenhil
1983	Lisa DeYoung, Kim Lautenbach, Judy Meyer, Sue Schaafsma
1990	Julie Bos, Denise Griffioen, Kelli Lautenbach, Gretchen Toxopeus, Lisa Visbeen
1991	Kendra Douma, Kelli Lautenbach-Schutte, Lisa Visbeen
1992	Melissa Dykstra, Shawn Farmer, Angie Feinauer, Kathy Haddox, Patsy Orkar, Tammy VanderPloeg
1993	Renea Bluekamp, Kendra Douma, Shawn Farmer, Angie Feinauer, Kathy Haddox, Becky Kuntzleman, Patsy Orkar
1994	Renea Bluekamp, Holly Breuker, Kendra Douma, Melissa Dykstra, Gwen Erffmeyer, Shawn Farmer, Kathy Haddox, Amy Kuipers, Esther Vahrmeyer
1995	Renea Bluekamp, Holly Breuker, Gwen Erffmeyer, Betsy Haverkamp, Amy Kuipers
1996	Holly Breuker, Amy Kuipers, Jennifer Rottschafer, Esther Vahrmeyer
1997	Betsy Haverkamp, Jennifer Rottschafer, Lisa Timmer
1998	Andrea Clark, Megan Pierce, Jennifer Rottschafer, Lisa Timmer, Kristi VanWoerkom, Sara Veltkamp
1999	Sarah Gritter, Lindsay Mulder, Megan Pierce, Kristi Van Woerkom, Sara Veltkamp
2000	Sarah Gritter, Lindsay Mulder, Megan Pierce, Sara Veltkamp, Mindy Worst
2001	Dana Haan, Lindsay Mulder, Megan Pierce, Annie Vander Laan, Sara Veltkamp, Mindy Worst
2002	Sue Abbring, Katie Corner, Laura Hamilton, Annie Vander Laan, Rachel Veltkamp, Mindy Worst
2003	Sue Abbring, Kristen Carlson, Katie Corner, Laura Hamilton, Christine Hendricks, Annie Vander Laan

Volleyball

1986	Julie Dykstra
1987	Leah Calsbeek, Julie Dykstra, Roxane Helmus
1997	Erika VanStralen
2000	Rhonda Volkers

143

LEAGUE AWARDS WON BY CALVIN ATHLETES

League Most Valuable Players

Following is a list of Calvin athletes who were voted MIAA MVP (Most Valuable Player), the year in which they received this honor, and the sport in which they participated.

Men's Baseball

1970 Mike Phelps
1975 Randy Wolthuis
1984 John Collier
2000 Aaron Wiers
2001 Aaron Wiers
2002 Jim Deters

Women's Basketball

1983 Sharon Boeve
1988 Julie Post
1993 Kim Bartman
1994 Pam Wubben
1999 Kerry Walters

Men's Basketball

1956 Don Vroon
1965 Ken Fletcher
1970 Mike Phelps
1971 Doug Taatjes
1974 Mark Veenstra
1975 Mark Veenstra
1976 Mark Veenstra
1977 Mark Veenstra
1980 Marty Grasmeyer

1986 Jim Schipper
1988 Dan Davis
1989 Dan Davis, Bill Sall
1990 Bill Sall
1992 Steve Honderd
1993 Steve Honderd
1994 Chris Knoester
1999 Aaron Winkle
2000 Aaron Winkle
2001 Jeremy Veenstra
2002 Jeremy Veenstra

Men's Cross Country

1978 Doug Diekema
1979 John Brink
1980 Doug Diekema
1982 John Brink
1987 Adam Suarez
1988 Adam Suarez
1989 Adam Suarez
1990 John Lumkes
1991 Thad Karnehm
1992 Ray Van Arragon,
         Derk Walkotten
1993 Ray Van Arragon
1994 Ray Van Arragon

1995 Geoff Van Dragt
1996 David Riemersma
1997 Kent Frens
1998 Geoff Van Dragt
1999 Joel Klooster
2000 Dan Hoekstra
2001 Justin Pfruender
2002 Hendrik Kok
2003 Dave Haagsma, Kris Koster

Women's Cross Country

1983 Laura Vroon
1989 Deb Vandersteen
1993 Renea Bluekamp
1994 Amy Kuipers
1995 Amy Kuipers
1996 Betsy Haverkamp
1997 Lisa Timmer
1998 Lisa Timmer
1999 Amy Mizzone
2000 Sarah Gritter
2001 Erinn Boot
2002 Jessie Lair
2003 Jessie Lair

Women's Field Hockey

1985 Lisa Reeder
1986 Lisa Reeder
1988 Leslie Tanis
1989 Jackie Vander Brug

Men's Golf

1965 Dave Tuls

Women's Soccer

1994 Kristin Penzotti
1997 Tara Dyk
2001 Tricia Dyk
2002 Tricia Dyk
2003 Sarah Weesies

Men's Soccer

1971 Don Buchholz
1972 Tom Van Tongeren
1973 Jim Johnson
1974 Tom Van Tongeren
1976 Roger King
1977 Mark Recker
1978 Mark Recker
1979 Mark Recker
1981 Doug DeSmit
1982 Doug DeSmit
1983 Doug DeSmit
1987 Dave Fasold
1989 Ed Wilgenburg
1991 Joey Barone
2000 Marcus Byeman

Women's Softball

1983 Sharon Boeve
1984 Sharon Boeve
1987 Jessica Schrier
1988 Anne Boshoven
1989 Laurie Hiemstra
1990 Kristi Klaasen
1996 Shauna Koolhaas
1997 Shauna Koolhaas,
         Melanie Bolt

Men's Swimming

1983 Steve Ruiter

Women's Swimming

2002 Katie Nagelkirk
2003 Katie Nagelkirk

Women's Tennis

1985 Tawnie Knottnerus

Women's Track and Field

1990 Kelli Lautenbach
1991 Kelli Lautenbach-Schutte
1993 Angie Feinauer
1994 Kathy Haddox
1996 Esther Vahrmeyer
1997 Betsy Haverkamp
1998 Jennifer Rottschafer
1999 Sarah Gritter, Megan Pierce
2000 Megan Pierce
2001 Lindsay Mulder,
         Megan Pierce
2002 Annie Vander Laan,
         Rachel Veltkamp
2003 Annie Vander Laan,
         Katie Corner

Men's Track and Field

1969 Rudy Vlaardingerbroek
1973 George Van Kampen
1974 Ben Beversluis
1990 John Lumkes
1991 David Sydow
1992 Thad Karnehm
1995 Ray Van Arragon
1996 J.D. Stien
1997 J.D. Stien
1998 Steve Michmerhuizen
1999 Phil Sikkenga
2000 Phil Sikkenga
2001 Phil Sikkenga
2002 Joel Klooster
2003 Nate Meckes

Women's Volleyball

1982 Deb VerHill
1984 Leah Calsbeek
1985 Julie Dykstra
1986 Leah Calsbeek, Julie Dykstra
1988 Amber Blankespoor
1989 Amber Blankespoor
1992 Betsy Wilgenburg
1996 Kristine DenHollander
1999 Rhonda Volkers
2000 Rhonda Volkers

All-MIAA Athletes

Following is a list of Calvin athletes who won All-MIAA honors during their years at Calvin, along with their sport and the year for which they were honored.

Men's Baseball

1954 Norm DeNooyer
1955 Stan Holthouse
1956 John Kloosterman,
    Arnie Rottman
1957 John DeMey, Len Holstege
1958 John DeMey
1959 Jerry Mulder
1960 Art Kraai
1961 Dan Bos
1962 Jim Kool, Jim Timmer
1963 Wayne Sikkenga
1964 Phil Van Slooten
1965 Jon Mulder
1966 Jim Goorman, Jon Mulder
1968 Buzz Wynbeek
1970 Paul Milkamp, Mike Phelps
1971 John Evenhouse,
    Dick Hatfield
1972 John Evenhouse,
    Dick Hatfield
1974 Jeff Sage, Gerry Sikkenga
1975 Jim DeGroot,
    Randy Wolthuis
1977 Jim Unrath
1980 Jim Snoeyink, Mark Stob,
    Mark Zietse

1981 Scott Hamstra, Steve Kraai
1982 Jeff Bartoszek
1983 Jeff Bartoszek
1984 John Collier, John Huizinga,
    Doug Ybema
1985 Joe Rinckey, Jim Schipper,
    Lon Sprecher,
    Kevin VanDuyn,
    Ken VerMeulen
1986 Jim Schipper, Kevin
    VanDuyn, Ken VerMeulen
1987 Kevin VanDuyn
1988 Lon Sprecher,
    Ken Stuursma
1989 Jim Timmer
1990 Bryan Ganzevoort
1991 Bryan Ganzevoort,
    Chris Knoester,
    Steve Ritsema
1992 Matt Rottman
1993 Steve Montsma, Jeff Timmer
1994 T.J. Cumings, Jeff Timmer
1995 T.J. Cumings, Jeff Timmer
1996 Tony DiLaura, Brad Dykstra,
    Mark Uyl
1997 Dan Mesyar
1998 Dan Mesyar

1999 Aaron Wiers
2000 Justin Cole, Steve Ekkens,
    Ross Hunderman,
    Mike Ott, Aaron Wiers
2001 Aaron Wiers
2002 Jim Deters, Ben Dykhouse,
    Arie Eppinga,
    Darrell Heuker,
    Josh Vriesman

Women's Basketball

1983 Sharon Boeve
1984 Judy Wasmer
1985 Amy Bierling
1988 Julie Post
1989 Karen Hiemstra
1991 Sarah Ondersma
1992 Kim Bartman
1993 Kim Bartman, Pam Wubben
1994 Pam Wubben
1995 Cheryl Essenburg,
    Stephanie Wiers
1996 Sara Burde,
    Stephanie Wiers
1997 Kerry Walters
1998 Mindi Andringa,
    Kerry Walters
1999 Mindi Andringa,
    Kerry Walters
2000 Mindi Andringa,
    Robyn Fennema

Men's Basketball

1954 Don Vroon
1955 Jim Kok, Don Vroon
1956 Jim Kok, Tom Newhof,
    Don Vroon
1958 Tom Newhof
1959 Ralph Honderd
1960 Bill Wolterstorff
1961 Carl DeKuiper,
    Ralph Honderd,
    Bill Wolterstorff
1962 Carl DeKuiper
1964 Ken Fletcher,
    Jim Van Eerden
1965 Ken Fletcher
1966 Bill De Horn
1967 Kim Campbell
1969 Mike Phelps, Ed Wiers
1970 Mike Phelps, Ed Wiers
1971 Doug Taatjes
1972 Art Tuls
1973 Art Tuls
1974 Larry Vander Veen,
    Mark Veenstra
1975 Marc Hoogewind,
    Larry Vander Veen,
    Mark Veenstra
1976 Mark Veenstra
1977 Barry Capel, Mark Veenstra
1978 Dwight Maliepaard
1980 Marty Grasmeyer

1981 Mark Grasmeyer
1982 Bruce Capel
1985 Kyle Vander Brug
1986 Jim Schipper,
Kevin VanDuyn
1987 Bill Sall, Kevin VanDuyn
1988 Dan Davis
1989 Dan Davis, Bill Sall
1990 Steve Honderd, Bill Sall
1991 Steve Honderd
1992 Steve Honderd,
Mark Lodewyk
1993 Steve Honderd,
Chris Knoester
1994 Chris Knoester,
Ryan Stevens,
Darrell VanLaare
1995 Brian Thwaites,
Darrell VanLaare
1996 Russ Iwema
1997 Russ Iwema
1998 Aaron Winkle
1999 Aaron Winkle
2000 Jeremy Veenstra,
Aaron Winkle
2001 Josh Tubergen,
Jeremy Veenstra
2002 Chris Prins, Jeremy Veenstra
2003 Jeremy Veenstra

Men's Cross Country

1964 Jack Bannink
1967 Jim Admiraal
1968 Bill Lautenbach
1969 Bill Lautenbach
1977 Doug Diekema
1978 Doug Diekema
1979 John Brink, Doug Diekema

1980 John Brink, Doug Diekema,
Kurt Mast
1981 John Brink, Kurt Mast
1982 John Brink, Kurt Mast,
Mike Verkaik
1983 Mike Kwantes
1985 Rick Admiraal
1986 Rick Admiraal,
Roosevelt Lee
1987 Rick Admiraal, John Lumkes,
Pat McNamara,
Adam Suarez
1988 Jeff Avery, John Lumkes,
Dwayne Masselink, Mike
Miedema, Adam Suarez
1989 Thad Karnehm, Dwayne
Masselink, Pat McNamara,
Adam Suarez,
David Sydow
1990 Rich Church, John Lumkes,
Thad Karnehm,
David Sydow
1991 Rich Church, Jim Hommes,
Thad Karnehm,
Keith Mulder, David Sydow
1992 Rich Church,
Brad Haverkamp,
Ryan LaFleur,
Matt Schellenberg,
Ray Van Arragon,
Derk Walkotten
1993 Wiebe Boer,
Brad Haverkamp,
Robert Hyde,
Ryan LaFleur,
Ray Van Arragon

1994 Wiebe Boer, Nate Dorn,
Robert Hyde,
Ryan LaFleur,
David Riemersma,
Ray Van Arragon
1995 Robert Hyde,
Ryan LaFleur, Nate Lewis,
David Riemersma,
Geoff Van Dragt,
Jason Washler
1996 Robert Hyde,
David Riemersma
1997 Jon Aukeman, Rob Bouws,
Lee Doherty, Kent Frens
1998 Lee Doherty, Paul Petersen,
Geoff Van Dragt,
Scott Westhouse
1999 Dan Hoekstra, Joel Klooster,
Paul Petersen
2000 Tim Avery,
Cameron Harrison,
Dan Hoekstra,
Joel Klooster, Kris Koster,
Justin Pfruender,
Paul Petersen
2001 Dan Hoekstra, Joel Klooster,
Kris Koster, Brian Maat,
Justin Pfruender,
David Ritsema,
Andy Yazzie
2002 Tim Avery, Jeff Engbers,
David Haagsma,
Hendrik Kok, Kris Koster,
Brian Maat, Brian Paff
2003 Tim Avery, Matt Edwards,
Jeff Engbers, Tim Finnegan,
Dave Haagsma,
Kris Koster, Andy Yazzie

Women's Cross Country

1982 Laura Vroon
1983 Laura Vroon
1984 Donna Hanenburg
1985 Donna Hanenburg
1986 Shelley DeWys,
Donna Hanenburg
1988 Dawn Harkema, Kim Talbot,
Shari Vander Horn,
Debbie Vander Steen
1989 Dawn Harkema, Kim Talbot,
Debbie Vander Steen
1990 Lisa Kuiper, Cindy Nieboer,
Kim Talbot
1991 Renea Bluekamp,
Laura Erffmeyer,
Becky Konyndyk,
Lisa Kuiper
1992 Laura Erffmeyer,
Amy Kuipers,
Heidi Lanning,
Amy Rideout
1993 Renea Bluekamp,
Betsy Haverkamp,
Amy Kuipers,
Amy Rideout
1994 Renea Bluekamp,
Betsy Haverkamp,
Korey Hofmann,
Amy Kuipers,
Amy Rideout
1995 Sara Gibson,
Betsy Haverkamp,
Amy Kuipers
1996 Andrea Clark,
Kristie DeYoung,
Betsy Haverkamp,
Erica Smith

1997 Rashel Bayes,
 Andrea Clark, Lisa Timmer
1998 Andrea Clark,
 Elizabeth Kuipers,
 Amy Mizzone, Lisa Timmer
1999 Rashel Bayes, Erinn Boot,
 Lindsay Carrier,
 Elizabeth Kuipers,
 Amy Mizzone,
 Lisa Timmer
2000 Erinn Boot,
 Lindsay Carrier,
 Sarah Gritter,
 Sarah Hastings,
 Jessie Lair,
 Laura Medema,
 Rashel Bayes Workman
2001 Rachel Baber, Ashley Berner,
 Erinn Boot, Sarah Hastings,
 Jessie Lair, Laura Medema,
 Mimi Speyer
2002 Sarah Hastings, Jessie Lair,
 Camille Medema,
 Jodi Vermeulen,
 Tami Vermeulen
2003 Sarah Hastings,
 Laura Holtrop, Jessie Lair,
 Camille Medema,
 Tami Vermeulen

Women's Field Hockey

1982 Kathleen Haun
1983 Laurie Russell
1984 Lisa Reeder, Barb Zoodsma
1985 Lisa Reeder, Leslie Tanis,
 Barb Zoodsma
1986 Lisa Reeder, Leslie Tanis,
 Lisa VanDellen

1987 Lisa Reeder, Leslie Tanis,
 Jackie Vander Brug
1988 Leslie Tanis, Karla Block,
 Teresa Cerrato,
 Jackie Vander Brug
1989 Jackie Vander Brug,
 Vera Magnuson,
 Deb Stout, Kara VanDellen
1990 Stacey Faber, Deb Stout,
 Kerin Sullivan, Kim Tanis

Women's Golf

1991 Kim Bartman

Men's Golf

1965 Dave Tuls, Paul Tuls
1966 Paul Tuls
1967 Dave Tuls
1970 Lloyd Dozeman
1972 Lloyd Dozeman
1980 Steve Kraai
1982 Steve Kraai
1986 Steve Ritsema
1988 Steve Ritsema
1989 Steve Ritsema
1991 Bruce Langerak
1992 Bruce Langerak
1994 Jeff Timmer
1996 Mark Van Stee
1997 Mark Van Stee
1999 Mark Van Stee
2000 Adam Derrickson
2001 Bryan Hoekstra,
 Jon Kalmink
2003 Phil Rietema

Women's Soccer

1989 Cheri Drukker,
 Gretchen Toxopeus
1990 Michelle Swierenga,
 Gretchen Toxopeus
1991 Michelle Swierenga,
 Melissa Van Heukelem
1992 Kristin Penzotti,
 Rebecca Reimink
1993 Kendra Douma,
 Kristin Penzotti
1994 Julie DeGraff,
 Kristin Penzotti
1995 Tara Dyk, Cindy Feinauer,
 Erin Henkel, Cara Jansen,
 Jennifer Sjoerdsma
1996 Tara Dyk, Cindy Feinauer,
 Erin Henkel, Cara Jansen
1997 Tara Dyk, Cara Jansen,
 Amber Wiersma
1998 Erin Cowell, Tara Dyk,
 Cara Jansen
1999 Tricia Dyk,
 Larissa Onderlinde,
 April Phelps
2000 Tricia Dyk, Dana Haan,
 April Phelps
2001 Tara Bergsma, Tricia Dyk
2002 Kristen Carlson, Tricia Dyk,
 Stephanie Kooima,
 Lindy VanHaitsma
2003 Noell Berghuis, Jill Capel,
 Sarah Weesies

Men's Soccer

1970 Don Buchholz,
 Ralph Fylstra, Jim Johnson,
 Tom Post, Bill Recker,
 Tom Weaver

1971 Don Buchholz,
 Don DeGraff, Jim Johnson,
 Tom Post, Bill Recker
1972 Bob Camp, Don DeGraff,
 Jim Johnson,
 Tom Van Tongeren
1973 Steve Bergman, Scott
 Bolkema, Jim Johnson,
 Tom Van Tongeren,
 Jerry Weesies
1974 Scott Bolkema,
 Jim Hengeveld, Roger King,
 Tom Van Tongeren,
 Jerry Weesies
1975 Jack Hertel, Roger King,
 Dan Pranger
1976 Roger King, Dan Pranger,
 Mark Recker
1977 Mark Recker,
 Don VanHeemst
1978 Don Cady, Mark Recker,
 Dave Ribbens,
 Don VanHeemst
1979 Eric Johnson, George Saa,
 Mark Recker, Mark Stacy
1980 Scott Hamstra, George Saa
1981 Doug DeSmit,
 Keith Saagman,
 Mark Schlenker, John Wilks
1982 Doug DeSmit,
 Keith Saagman, John Wilks
1983 Doug DeSmit, John Wilks
1984 Dave Lindner,
 Ken Lodewyk,
 Bob Nykamp
1985 Bert Bowden, Ed Glas,
 David Lindner

1986 Bert Bowden,
    Mark Hendriks,
    Butch Hubers,
    Tim Messmer
1987 Bert Bowden, Dave Fasold,
    Stanley Hielema,
    Jeff Veenhuis,
    Tom Wybenga
1988 Joey Barone, Don Miller,
    Jeff Veenhuis,
    Ed Wilgenburg
1989 Joey Barone, Dave Stokes,
    Todd Veenhuis,
    Ed Wilgenburg
1990 Joey Barone, Chris Hughes,
    Todd Veenhuis,
    Ed Wilgenburg
1991 Joey Barone, Jon Heun,
    Jeremy Klop, Chris Riker,
    Todd Veenhuis
1992 Jon Heun, Joel Nieuwenhuis
1993 Wayne Huizinga,
    Trevor Schuurman,
    Julius Siebenga
1994 Dan Schuurman,
    Kevin Sowles
1995 Daryl Michael,
    Steve Wiegers
1996 Steve Wiegers
1997 Steve Wiegers
1998 Marcus Byeman,
    Mark Lindner
1999 Marcus Byeman,
    Todd Folkert,
    Peter Knoester,
    Jake Wisner
2000 Marcus Byeman,
    Jason DeJonge,
    Peter Knoester

2002 Joel Vande Kopple,
    Joel Veldhouse, Kurt Visker
2003 Joel Vande Kopple,
    Joel Veldhouse, Kurt Visker

Women's Softball

1983 Sharon Boeve,
    Pam Lancaster,
    Janna TerMolen,
    Laura Vroon
1984 Sharon Boeve,
    Janna TerMolen,
    Laura Vroon
1985 Sharon Boeve,
    Sherri Maring
1986 Linda DeWeerd,
    Jessica Schrier,
    Marci Tawney
1987 Roxane Helmus,
    Laurie Hiemstra,
    Jessica Schrier
1988 Anne Boshoven,
    Doretta Diekman,
    Laurie Hiemstra,
    Chris Pscodna
1989 Anne Boshoven,
    Laurie Hiemstra,
    Kristi Klaasen,
    Sarah Ondersma,
    Heidi Rottman
1990 Laurie Hiemstra,
    Kristi Klaasen,
    Heidi Rottman
1991 Julie Overway
1992 Julie Overway
1994 Brooke Doornbos,
    Holly Ondersma

1995 Shauna Koolhaas,
    Holly Ondersma,
    Laurie Pettinga
1996 Melanie Harriff,
    Shauna Koolhaas,
    Cheryl VanderKamp
1997 Melanie Bolt,
    Melanie Harriff,
    Shauna Koolhaas
1998 Shauna Koolhaas,
    Marissa VanKoevering,
    Rhonda Volkers
1999 Sara Plasman,
    Rhonda Volkers
2000 Susannah Knust,
    Sara Plasman
2001 Erin Dyksterhouse
2002 Laurel Sands
2003 Jeanne Cole,
    Rachelle Heyboer

Women's Swimming

1983 Mary Otter, Deb Ruiter,
    Cathy Vila, Cheryl Weaver
1984 Mary Otter, Deb Ruiter,
    Cheryl Weaver
1985 Sari Brummel,
    Karen Dekker, Mary Otter,
    Liesl VandeCreek,
    Cathy Vila
1986 Sari Brummel,
    Anita Haynal,
    Liesl VandeCreek
1987 Sari Brummel, Liesl Pruis,
    Stephanie Rhind
1988 Laura Lantinga, Liesl Pruis,
    Stephanie Rhind

1989 Jacki Belyea,
    Stephanie Rhind,
    Patti Van Andel
1990 Jacki Belyea, Stephanie
    Rhind, Patti Van Andel,
    Miriam Vos
1991 Jacki Belyea
1993 Jennifer Cole
1994 Kathleen Shaughnessy
1996 Kristi VanWoerkom
1997 Leslie Harris,
    Kristi Van Woerkom
1998 Kristi Van Woerkom
1999 Kara Davidson,
    Liesje Konyndyk,
    Erin Kloostra, Erica Smith,
    Kristi VanWoerkom
2000 Ginni Baker, Kate Conrad,
    Liesje Konyndyk,
    Erin Kloostra, Anne Kuiper,
    Katie Nagelkirk
2001 Ginni Baker,
    Kate Conrad,
    Erin Kloostra,
    Liesje Konyndyk,
    Anne Kuiper,
    Mara McGuin,
    Katie Nagelkirk
2002 Kate Conrad,
    Erin Kloostra,
    Mara McGuin,
    Katie Nagelkirk,
    Brittney Stevens
2003 Abby Johnson, Anne Kuiper,
    Katie Nagelkirk,
    Brittney Stevens,
    Sara TerHaar, Lynn Visser

Men's Swimming

1972 Dave Follett
1973 Rick Feenstra
1974 Rick Steenwyk
1975 Ken Mange, Rick Steenwyk
1976 Dave Cooke, Rick Feenstra,
     Ken Koldenhoven,
     Dave Otten
1977 Jim Mange, Dave Otten,
     Robert Reehoorn
1978 Jim Mange,
     Robert Reehoorn,
     Tom Tabor
1979 Robert Reehoorn
1980 Robert Reehoorn
1981 Dirk Pruis
1982 Dirk Pruis
1983 Steve Ruiter
1984 Steve Ruiter
1985 Steve Ruiter,
     Charlie Vander Ploeg
1986 Eric Danhof, Steve Ruiter,
     Charlie Vander Ploeg
1987 Charlie Vander Ploeg
1988 Eric Danhof,
     Charlie Vander Ploeg
1990 Jeff Homan, Tom Marks
1991 Alex Porte
1993 Mike Lubbers
1994 Mike Lubbers
1995 Mike Lubbers,
     Mike Shoemaker
1996 Mike Lubbers,
     Mike Shoemaker,
     Mike Vander Baan
1997 Dave Baron, Keith Ritsema,
     Mike Vander Baan
1998 Brad Flikkema,

Brad Rietema,
Keith Ritsema,
Mike Vander Baan
1999 Brad Flikkema,
     Mike Vander Baan
2000 A.J. Penninga
2001 A.J. Penninga, Chris Veltman,
     Brad White
2002 Peter Boumgarden,
     A.J. Penninga, Brad White
2003 Peter Boumgarden,
     Ryan Johnson,
     A.J. Penninga, Brad White

Men's Tennis

1967 Bert DeLeeuw,
     Ben Pekelder
1968 Ben Pekelder
1970 Ben Pekelder,
     Mark Van Faasen
1973 Greg Broene
1977 Dean Ellens, Dave Hartman
1978 Dave Hartman
1979 Dave Hartman
1980 Dave Hartman
1990 Mark Lenters
1991 Alex Vander Pol
1992 John Knoester, Brad Sytsma
1993 John Knoester, Brad Sytsma
1994 John Knoester
1995 Steve DeWeerd,
     John Knoester
1996 Steve DeWeerd
1997 Jeff VanNoord
1998 Dave Meester
2002 Kevin Van Haitsma
2003 Kevin Van Haitsma

Women's Tennis

1983 Jan Boerema,
     Carol Vorenkamp
1984 Jan Boerema,
     Tawnie Knottnerus
1985 Tawnie Knottnerus
1986 Sue Penning
1991 Denise Koopman,
     Betty Williams
1992 Betty Williams
1993 Debbie Pettinga
1995 Alison DeWys
1996 Alison DeWys
1997 Alison DeWys
1998 Alison DeWys
1999 Amanda Sytsma
2000 Kait Disselkoen,
     Katie Zeilstra
2001 Kait Disselkoen
2002 Sally Skodinski
2003 Sally Skodinski

Women's Track and Field

1983 Amy Bierling, Lori DuBois,
     Kim Lautenbach,
     Sue Schaafsma
1984 Lisa DeYoung, Laura Vroon,
     Barb Zoodsma
1985 Donna Hanenburg,
     Tammy Oostendorp,
     Barb Zoodsma
1986 Kristin Hiemstra,
     Patty O'Hara,
     Donna VanderVeen
1987 Diane DeBoer,
     Deb VanderSteen,
     Donna VanderVeen
1988 Jacqueline Hacquebord,

Kelli Lautenbach,
Deb VanderSteen,
Donna VanderVeen
1989 Kelli Lautenbach,
     Annette Post, Deb Vander-
     Steen, Donna VanderVeen
1990 Julie Bos, Shelley DeWys,
     Mary Gootjes,
     Kelli Lautenbach,
     Lisa Visbeen
1991 Kendra Douma,
     Angie Feinauer,
     Mary Gootjes,
     Denise Griffioen,
     Kelli Lautenbach-Schutte,
     Lisa Visbeen
1992 Renea Bluekamp,
     Kendra Douma,
     Laura Erffmeyer,
     Shawn Farmer,
     Angie Feinauer,
     Kathy Haddox,
     Becky Konyndyk
1993 Renea Bluekamp,
     Holly Breuker,
     Kendra Douma,
     Gwen Erffmeyer,
     Shawn Farmer,
     Angie Feinauer,
     Kathy Haddox,
     Amy Kuipers,
     Becky Kuntzleman,
     Patsy Orkar,
     Betsy Wilgenburg
1994 Renea Bluekamp,
     Alayna Bockheim,
     Holly Breuker,
     Kendra Douma,
     Kristin Douma,

Melissa Dykstra,
Gwen Erffmeyer,
Shawn Farmer,
Kathy Haddox,
Betsy Haverkamp,
Kristin Heeringa,
Amy Kuipers,
Esther Vahrmeyer

1995 Renea Bluekamp,
Holly Breuker,
Kristin Douma,
Gwen Erffmeyer,
Kathy Haddox,
Betsy Haverkamp,
Amy Kuipers,
Esther Vahrmeyer

1996 Holly Breuker,
Andrea Clark,
Kristie DeYoung,
Kristin Douma,
Gwen Erffmeyer,
Jami Kimm, Amy Kuipers,
Kelly Peterson,
Esther Vahrmeyer,
Ann Zylstra

1997 Andrea Clark,
Kristie DeYoung,
Betsy Haverkamp, Jami
Kimm, Kim Mejeur,
Amy Mizzone,
Jennifer Rottschafer,
Lisa Timmer,
Kristi VanWoerkom

1998 Andrea Clark,
Sarah Gritter,
Amy Mizzone,
Megan Pierce, Lisa Timmer,
Teresa Timmer,
Sara Veltkamp

1999 Carrie Anderson,
Mandy Gretzinger,
Sarah Gritter,
Lindsay Mulder,
Megan Pierce,
Teresa Timmer,
Rachel Veltkamp,
Sara Veltkamp

2000 Rashel Bayes, Liz Blevins,
Erinn Boot, Sarah Gritter,
Liz Kuipers,
Lindsay Mulder,
Megan Pierce, Andrea Rip,
Lisa Timmer,
Annie Vander Laan,
Anna VanDrie,
Rachel Veltkamp,
Sara Veltkamp,
Mindy Worst,
Bethany Zylstra

2001 Mae Baber, Lindsay Carrier,
Leah Cornell, Jamie Febo,
Dana Haan, Jessie Lair,
Laura Medema,
Lindsay Mulder,
Megan Pierce, Andrea Rip,
Annie Vander Laan,
Rachel Veltkamp, Sarah
Veltkamp, Mindy Worst

2002 Sue Abbring, Erinn Boot,
Lindsay Carrier,
Katie Corner, Sara Crowe,
Laura Hamilton,
Sarah Hastings, Jessie Lair,
Mandy Van Den Bosch,
Annie Vander Laan,
Rachel Veltkamp,
Tami Vermeulen,
Mindy Worst

2003 Sue Abbring, Katie Corner,
Laura Hamilton,
Sarah Hastings,
Christine Hendricks,
Jessie Lair,
Camille Medema,
Missy Smith,
Annie Vander Laan,
Kim Vanderzee,
Mandy Van Den Bosch,
Jodi Vermeulen,
Tami Vermeulen

Men's Track and Field

1965 Ben Snoeyink, Jim Wynstra,
Dave VerMerris
1966 Bill DeHorn, Stan Klop,
Dave VerMerris
1967 Dave Heth, Dave VerMerris,
Rudy Vlaardingerbroek
1968 Jack Vander Male,
Dave VerMerris,
Rudy Vlaardingerbroek
1969 Larry Baar,
Jack Vander Male,
Rudy Vlaardingerbroek
1970 Joel Vander Male
1971 Larry Baar, John Rottschafer,
Randy Veltkamp
1972 John DeJonge,
Randy Veltkamp
1973 Ron Bosch, John DeJonge,
Larry Terborg,
Ron VanderPol,
George VanKampen
1974 Gregg Afman,
Ben Beversluis,
Gary Veurink

1975 Gregg Afman, Gary Veurink
1976 Gregg Afman,
Jon Houseward,
Gary Mulder,
Randy Veenstra,
Gary Veurink
1977 Dave Alkema,
Jon Houseward,
Gary Mulder,
John VanderKamp,
Randy Veenstra
1978 Dave Alkema, Jim Busscher,
Ron Cok, Jon Houseward,
John VanderKamp,
Randy Veenstra
1979 Ron Cok, Doug Diekema,
Jon Houseward,
John VanderKamp
1980 Ron Cok, Tim Hoekstra,
Dave Tuuk
1981 John Brink, Doug Diekema,
John Hart, Tim Hoekstra,
Dave Tuuk
1982 John Brink, Kurt Mast
1983 Mike Kwantes, Kurt Mast,
Duane Wolterstorff
1984 Dan Diekema,
Mike Kwantes, Bill Veurink
1985 Dan Diekema,
Chris Holstege,
Bob Kamps,
Todd Vandenberg
1986 Ken DeGraaf,
Chris Holstege,
Randy Ritsema,
Pete VandeBrake
1987 Troy Billin, Ken DeGraaf,
Bob Feyen, Ryan Lubbers,

Todd Vandenberg,
Pete VandeBrake,
Dean Vander Hill

1988 Mark Haan, Chris Holstege,
Ryan Lubbers,
John Lumkes,
Pat McNamara,
Dan Owen,
Robb Steenwyk,
Pete VandeBrake,
Norman Zylstra

1989 Rick Lubbers, Ryan Lubbers,
John Lumkes, Dan Owen,
Robb Steenwyk,
Dave Sydow, Vince Woltjer

1990 Brian Davis, Thad Karnehm,
Rick Lubbers,
Ryan Lubbers,
John Lumkes,
Robb Steenwyk,
David Sydow,
Vince Woltjer

1991 Tom Broene,
Richard Church,
Thad Karnehm,
Rick Lubbers,
Robb Steenwyk,
David Sydow, Craig Tanis

1992 Thad Karnehm,
Rick Lubbers, Steve Seth,
David Sydow

1993 Rich Church, Greg Helmer,
Ryan LaFleur, Steve Seth,
Mark VerMerris,
Derk Walkotten,
Steve Witvoet

1994 Greg Helmer, Ryan LaFleur,
Matt Schellenberg,
Ray Van Arragon,

Mark VerMerris,
Matt Winkle,
Steve Witvoet

1995 Scott Postma, Earle Seinen,
J.D. Stien,
Ray Van Arragon,
Mark VerMerris,
Matt Winkle

1996 Brett Hamilton,
Ryan LaFleur, Nate Lewis,
Jay Lumkes,
Pete Overvoorde,
David Riemersma,
Earle Seinen, J.D. Stien

1997 Scott Buyze, Lee Doherty,
Jonathan Lefers,
Nathan Lewis, Jay Lumkes,
Steve Michmerhuizen,
Scott Postma,
David Riemersma,
J.D. Stien

1998 Mark DeWeerd,
Lee Doherty, Kent Frens,
Jay Lumkes,
Steve Michmerhuizen,
Curt Mulder, Phil Sikkenga,
Geoff Van Dragt

1999 Mark De Weerd,
Lee Doherty,
Dan Hoekstra,
Derek Kleinheksel,
Nate Kuipers, Jay Lumkes,
Steve Michmerhuizen,
Curt Mulder, Phil Sikkenga,
Keith Van Goor

2000 Mark DeWeerd,
Eric Hansen,
Derek Kleinheksel,
Joel Klooster,

Bryan Mayhew,
Justin Pfruender,
Paul Petersen,
Phil Sikkenga,
Keith Van Goor,
Scott Westhouse

2001 Cameron Baron,
Mark DeWeerd,
Dave Haagsma,
Dan Hoekstra,
Derek Kleinheksel,
Justin Pfruender,
Paul Petersen,
David Ritsema,
Phil Sikkenga

2002 Steve Abbring,
Pete Armstrong,
Cameron Baron,
Dave Haagsma,
Dan Hoekstra,
Jonathan Hutchful,
Joel Klooster, Hendrik Kok,
Brian Maat, Nate Meckes,
Ryan Moore,
Justin Pfruender,
Keith Van Goor

2003 Tim Avery, Cameron Baron,
Dave Haagsma,
Jonathan Hutchful,
Francis Ikwueme,
Joel Klooster, Hendrik Kok,
Nate Meckes, Andy Yazzie

Women's Volleyball

1982 Lynn Bolt, Deb VerHill
1983 Lynn Bolt, Leah Calsbeek
1984 Lynn Bolt, Leah Calsbeek,
Kathy DeHaan

1985 Leah Calsbeek,
Kathy DeHaan,
Julie Dykstra,
Kim Lautenbach

1986 Leah Calsbeek,
Julie Dykstra,
Roxane Helmus

1987 Amber Blankespoor,
Laurel Calsbeek

1988 Amber Blankespoor,
Laurel Calsbeek

1989 Amber Blankespoor,
Kris Speidel

1990 Pam Van Tol

1991 Pam Van Tol,
Christen Veltman

1992 Pam Van Tol,
Christen Veltman,
Betsy Wilgenburg

1993 Rachel Schepel,
Christy Keen

1994 Kristine DenHollander

1995 Kristine DenHollander,
Erika Van Stralen

1996 Kristine DenHollander,
Jill Harkema,
Erika Van Stralen

1997 Erin Hall, Erika Van Stralen

1998 Erin Hall, Charla Holmes,
Rhonda Volkers

1999 Sara Arenholz,
Charla Holmes,
Rhonda Volkers

2000 Sara Ahrenholz,
Rhonda Volkers

2001 Sara Ahrenholz, Melissa Pell

2002 Melissa Pell, Laura Tucker

2003 Trisha Balkema,
Kara Kuipers

EPILOGUE

Fifty years is a half-century and thus represents a sizable span of time. It is my hope that the students and alumni who have read this attempt to chronicle those years have done so with pleasure.

It is also my hope that the student-athletes of the next 50 years be just as dedicated and successful as those of the past.

Calvin College has first-rate athletic facilities, but more importantly, has caring Christian coaches. May the Christian spirit they project continue to be evident in all aspects of Calvin's athletic program.

It is a privilege to be part of the Maroon and Gold tradition, whether one is an athlete or fan.

May God bless the future of the college so many of us have come to love.

David B. Tuuk